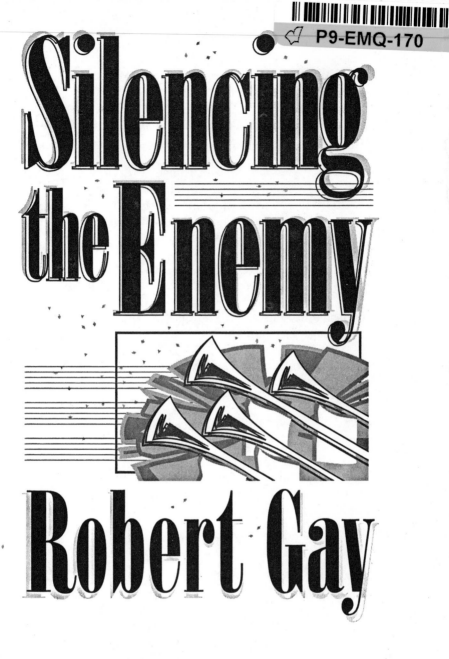

Silencing the Enemy

Robert Gay

CREATION HOUSE

BOOKS ABOUT SPIRIT-LED LIVING

ORLANDO, FLORIDA

Creation House
Strang Communications Company
600 Rinehart Road
Lake Mary, FL 32746
Phone: (407) 333-3132

Unless otherwise noted, all Scripture quotations are
from the King James Version of the Bible.

Scripture quotations marked NIV are from the Holy Bible,
New International Version. Copyright © 1973, 1978, 1984,
International Bible Society. Used by permission.

First printing, August 1993
Second printing, October 1993
Third printing, April 1994
Fourth printing, August 1994
Fifth printing, March 1995

*This book is dedicated especially
to my beautiful wife, Stacey,
and my three children,
Joshua, Kayla and Micah.
I love you all very dearly.
Thank you for supporting me
during the writing of this book
while I worked what seemed
at times to be endless hours.
You are a great source
of inspiration to me.
May all the body of Christ
also be grateful to you
for your love and sacrifice
that no one else sees but me.*

CONTENTS

The contents of this book can revolutionize your life and activate you to become a mighty warrior in the army of Jesus Christ. God wants His present-day church to understand and use the great weapon of war that is being revealed. He wants His voice to be heard as His church arises to subdue and silence all His enemies. God's warrior-saints are the court bailiffs to execute His prison sentences against the devil and his evil empire.

Jesus Christ is the same yesterday, today and forever, and His written Word does not change. Yet He continually brings forth fresh illumination of His Word and revelation of His character. *Silencing the Enemy* reveals God's warrior nature. It brings new understanding about the power of praise and worship.

Protestant movement songwriters extolled God's great mercy in providing salvation through grace and faith. The Holiness movement songwriters exalted God's holiness and the second coming of Christ. The Pentecostal movement singers praised God for His supernatural works, entering into praise in response to what they saw, heard or felt. The charismatic movement chorus writers praised God for His greatness, liberty, joy and provisions. They praised God to bring forth His presence. Now the prophet minstrels in the prophetic movement are praising with further revelation of God's purpose for praise.

Robert Gay has been called to be a prophetic minstrel in the body of Christ. When he came among the company of prophets at Christian International, the revelation and anointing of God activated him to write the words and melodies establishing warfare praise in the church. Warfare praise is one of eight major truths and ministries being restored in the prophetic movement.

One of the seven principles found in every major restorational move of God is that new songs, choruses and music will be brought forth with new words and melodies that portray the message and ministry coming forth in that movement.[1]

Robert Gay has been commissioned by the Holy

Spirit to make known the new dimension of worship and warfare praise coming forth in the church. Christian International Network of Prophetic Ministries has preached and practiced warfare praise in our local churches and conferences for over five years, testifying to its biblical validity. The results have been outstanding victories, souls saved, bodies healed, church growth, prosperity and even whole nations influenced for God.

Warfare praise has proven to be a great and effective offensive weapon for the church against the flood of witchcraft, satanism, the occult and New Agers. Warfare praise is a standard that God is raising up against this flood.

As you read this book please pray the prayer of Ephesians 1:16-23. Allow the Spirit of revelation to cause your eyes to be enlightened so that you may know the greatness of His power toward those who believe — not only in Jesus, but in His dynamic principle of warfare praise. Let us use our powerful aggressive weapon of warfare praise to silence the enemy.

Bill Hamon
Founder and president
Christian International
   Network of Prophetic Ministries

THE EVOLUTION OF PRAISE AND WORSHIP

Music and worship have played an integral role in the church throughout history. A study of church music and worship reveals that God has restored different elements of worship progressively. He has led the church from glory to glory through fresh revelation from heaven. As the church was changed and conformed to what God was saying in times past, so we must change and conform to what He is saying today.

God uses a person to proclaim the revelation which the Spirit is illuminating to the church. The unfolding of this revelation to the body of Christ becomes known as a move of God. Paralleling this, He also raises up psalmists to write songs that embody the truths of that movement. Thus, He enhances every movement through the use of music and worship.

An in-depth study of church history also illustrates that with every move of God came changes in the way worship was expressed. Along with new songs, other expressions of worship became more demonstrative. Musical instruments considered "taboo" by a previous generation were brought into the church.

The church in recent years has seen a tremendous growth in the emphasis of praise and worship. More tapes, books, seminars and manuals have been produced on this subject in the last decade than in the entire history of the church. I personally have had the experience of writing songs for Integrity's Hosanna! Music for the past four years.

All this activity indicates that once again the wind of the Spirit is blowing throughout the earth to usher in fresh insight, revelation and experiences, accompanied by new songs, choruses and expressions of worship. A distinct emphasis on particular aspects of praise and worship will take us to a higher realm of glory and a new experience with God. He has prepared new garments for us to wear in our generation. The Spirit of God is bidding us to come up a little higher.

Today a fresh sound is coming forth. God is raising up men and women who are writing songs to bring the church to attention. These songs are teaching and admonishing us with the truths concerning spiritual warfare. God is raising up prophetic songwriters to bring forth the war songs of Zion so the church may become the fighting army He has called it to be.

Jesus said that His church would be built upon the rock (Matt. 16:18). He went on to say that as the church is built upon that rock, the gates of hell would not prevail against it. The ministry of praise and worship must be built upon a rock of revelation-knowledge.

The Bible says that the people of God are destroyed for a lack of knowledge (Hos. 4:6). Without a revelation of what God is saying concerning worship in this hour, we will be like the children of Israel who wandered in the wilderness for forty years and died. But as we joyfully receive and enter into the revelation of the Spirit, we will be like those who crossed the Jordan and obtained their promised possession. Let us not be a generation of wilderness walkers but rather Canaan conquerors!

Our praise is a weapon of war, and God has a prophetic purpose for establishing praise and worship in the church. As you read and study this book, allow the Holy Spirit to birth the truths contained here in your heart. As you do, I believe your life will be changed.

ONE

GOD'S PROPHETIC PURPOSE FOR PRAISE

A mos prophesied by the Spirit about a time when God would restore the tabernacle of David.

> In that day I will restore David's fallen tent. I will repair its broken places, restore its ruins, and build it as it used to be, so that they may possess... (Amos 9:11-12, NIV).

David's fallen tent refers to what has become known as the tabernacle of David. Let me define briefly what that constituted.

In 1 Chronicles 16 we read the account of the origin of David's tabernacle. We can see from Scripture that this was a place of praise. Inside David's tabernacle was the ark of the covenant, and before the ark the priests gave continual praise, worship and thanks. It was a place of joy where music resounded in honor of Jehovah God.

> They brought the ark of God and set it inside the tent that David had pitched for it, and they presented burnt offerings and fellowship offerings before God...He appointed some of the Levites to minister before the ark of the Lord, to make petition, to give thanks, and to praise the Lord, the God of Israel: Asaph was the chief, Zechariah second, then Jeiel, Shemiramoth, Jehiel, Mattithiah, Eliab, Benaiah, Obed-Edom and Jeiel. They were to play the lyres and harps. Asaph was to sound the cymbals, and Benaiah and Jahaziel the priests were to blow the trumpets regularly before the ark of the covenant of God (vv. 1,4-6, NIV).

We can easily see that the tabernacle of David was a place where God was continually praised and worshipped. In the Old Testament it was the ultimate place of worship — a place of continual praise.

Hundreds of years later after the removal of David's tabernacle, Amos writes that a day is coming when God will restore the tabernacle of David and build it as it used to be. To understand what the Spirit of God is saying through the prophet Amos, let's first address what He is not saying.

The Holy Spirit is not telling us there will be a literal, physical restoration of the tabernacle of David. The ark of the covenant will not be placed in a tent again. Neither will we board a 747 jet and go to Jerusalem to worship. When the woman at the well (John 4) asked where to worship, Jesus told her clearly that true worship was determined not by geographical location but by heart attitude and obedience to the Word of God.

The Spirit of God is revealing through Amos that a day is coming when the priestly and spiritual ministry of worship that was conducted in David's tabernacle will be restored. I believe that day is right now!

The church today is experiencing a revival of praise and worship. Why? Is it a fad? No, it is rather that we are living in the day when God is restoring the tabernacle of David.

GOD HAS A PURPOSE

God has a purpose for everything He does. He never does anything without a reason. By understanding His purpose, we can become part of His plan.

The Bible tells us why God sent Jesus to earth. "For this *purpose* the Son of God was manifested, that he might destroy the works of the devil" (1 John 3:8, emphasis added). Likewise, God has a purpose for restoring the tabernacle of David.

When we tell our children to do something, they

may respond with the question why. We often answer, "Because I said so!" That alone is a good enough reason for them to do what we tell them to. But at times it is a good idea to let them know why. If we tell them not to put their fingers in electrical outlets or not to play in the middle of the street, they should know the reason — that they could get killed if they do! Your children may thereby be persuaded that "to obey is better than sacrifice" (1 Sam. 15:22).

Now God is a loving heavenly Father and knows that man has a desire to have a purpose. He has placed that desire within us. Therefore, He gives us reasons for the restoration of the tabernacle of David involving praise and worship. After Amos declares that God is going to restore and rebuild the tabernacle of David, God's purpose for the restoration is revealed: "so that they may possess..." (9:12, NIV). Here we see God's prophetic purpose for the restoration of the ministry of praise and worship: possessing.

To understand what is being communicated we must first define the word *possess*. This is the Hebrew word *yaresh* which means to "occupy by driving out the previous tenants, to cast out, to consume, to destroy, to disinherit." God is restoring the tabernacle of David so that the church will have an instrument of warfare to drive out, cast out, consume and destroy the works of darkness, disinherit the devil and occupy the earth. Hallelujah! Jesus was manifested for the same reason that praise and worship are being restored — to destroy the works of the devil.

AN EXAMPLE OF POSSESSING

Not long ago, America was engaged with the nation of Iraq in a military conflict known as the Gulf War and Operation Desert Storm. The primary reason for this war was that Iraq had illegally invaded and taken over the nation of Kuwait.

Although the United Nations Security Council issued resolutions to the nation of Iraq stating that Iraq had acted illegally and must withdraw its troops from Kuwait, Saddam Hussein, the leader of Iraq, chose to ignore the resolutions. That meant one thing: for the people of Kuwait to repossess their land, their enemy (the Iraqi army) would have to be driven out. In other words, war was inevitable because their enemy would not voluntarily get out of their country.

The offensive plan of Operation Desert Storm drove out the Iraqi army physically. To repossess Kuwait, it took an offensive, physical, aggressive act of war. We were not there just to defend Israel, Saudi Arabia and the other surrounding countries. We were there to possess by driving out the previous tenants.

Our enemy Satan is even more lawless than Saddam Hussein. The devil will not voluntarily give you back what he has stolen from you. Jesus said, "The thief comes only to steal" (John 10:10). For the Israelites to possess Canaan, they had to go to war. To possess what is promised to you, you will have to enter into spiritual warfare. Remember, Canaan is a type of the blessings of God that have been promised and even given to you. But just like the Israelites, you will have to go to war to take full possession and occupy your land.

The apostle Paul writes, "For the weapons of our warfare are not carnal, but mighty through God to the pulling down of strong holds" (2 Cor. 10:4). He also writes, "For we wrestle [war] not against flesh and blood, but against principalities" (Eph. 6:12). We must understand that the Bible teaches that we, the church, are to enter into spiritual warfare and fight with spiritual weapons.

Praise is one of the weapons God has given us. It is not a carnal weapon but a spiritual weapon of war. God is restoring the tabernacle of David today. He is restoring the priestly ministry of praise, and we are to enter into it "so that [we] may possess." It is so that we, the church, may drive out our enemy, the devil, and receive our rightful inheritance.

TWO

OUT OF THE MOUTH OF BABES

*From the lips of children and infants
you have ordained praise,
because of your enemies,
to silence the foe and the avenger.*
Psalm 8:2, NIV

As stated earlier, God has a purpose for everything He does. Thus far we have discovered God's purpose for restoring the tabernacle of David: so we may have a weapon of warfare to drive out the forces of darkness and take possession of what God has given to us.

Have you ever wondered why God commands and desires our praise? Is it because He has an ego problem? Is He insecure? Does He need our praise? The answer to all these questions is emphatically no. God is not insecure, even though we would consider someone who needed continual praise to be insecure. God does not need our praise. Scripture records that there are creatures in heaven that do nothing but worship Him day and night (Rev. 4:8).

Why then has God ordained our praise? Psalm 8:2 gives us the answer: "because of our enemies." Some people feel they have done the Lord a great service if they spend thirty minutes worshipping Him. The fact is we do not do Him a favor; we do ourselves a favor and the devil great damage. God has not ordained praise because He needs it, but because *we need to praise Him.*

Ezekiel refers to Lucifer as "the anointed cherub."

> Thou hast been in Eden the garden of God; every precious stone was thy covering, the sardius, topaz, and the diamond, the beryl, the onyx, and the jasper, the sapphire, the emerald, and the carbuncle, and gold: the workmanship of thy tabrets and of thy pipes was prepared in thee in the day that thou wast created. Thou art the anointed cherub that covereth; and I have set thee so (Ezek. 28:13-14).

Lucifer was called to lead all of heaven in worship to the most high God. He was a "one-man band" with instruments built into his body. He was a masterpiece fashioned and formed for the purposes of God. But Lucifer fell because of pride.

How art thou fallen from heaven, O Lucifer, son of the morning! how art thou cut
down to the ground, which didst weaken
the nations! For thou hast said in thine
heart, I will ascend into heaven, I will exalt my throne above the stars of God: I will
sit also upon the mount of the congregation, in the sides of the north: I will ascend
above the heights of the clouds; I will be
like the most High. Yet thou shalt be
brought down to hell, to the sides of the pit
(Is. 14:12-15).

Because of a prideful heart, Satan fell from
heaven, lost his heavenly anointing and was cast
to the earth. He had not rightly discerned the call,
anointing and gift God had given to him. God had
given him a glorious ministry, a ministry that was
to bring all heaven into a united symphony of
praise unto the Lord. His ministry was one that
would cause him to live in the presence of God
before His throne continually. He would have had
the privilege of being known as God's most beautiful creation. But iniquity was found in him, and he
lost it all.

By the multitude of thy merchandise they
have filled the midst of thee with violence,
and thou hast sinned: therefore I will cast
thee as profane out of the mountain of
God: and I will destroy thee, O covering
cherub, from the midst of the stones of
fire. Thine heart was lifted up because of
thy beauty, thou hast corrupted thy wisdom by reason of thy brightness: I will

cast thee to the ground, I will lay thee before kings, that they may behold thee. Thou hast defiled thy sanctuaries by the multitude of thine iniquities, by the iniquity of thy traffic; therefore will I bring forth a fire from the midst of thee, it shall devour thee, and I will bring thee to ashes upon the earth in the sight of all them that behold thee (Ezek. 28:16-18).

The good news is that the devil's loss was our gain! I think God turned to the devil and said something like this, "I gave you a glorious ministry, yet you became consumed with yourself rather than Me. You disdained the ministry that I gave you, and because of this I revoke your heavenly anointing and heavenly position, and you will be cast down to the ground.

"As further punishment to you, I will take the ministry of praise and worship that you forsook and give it to a group of people on the earth that shall be known as the church. Every time they enter into this ministry of worship, the ministry that you forsook, they will silence and paralyze you. They will take up the ministry of praise and worship and with it bind you, break you, bruise you and ultimately destroy your kingdom!"

The wonderful thing God did was to take what Satan was originally anointed to do and allow us, the body of Christ, to use it as a weapon of warfare to destroy his plans.

Psalm 8:2 says that God has ordained praise because of our enemy, to silence the avenger. The word *silence* is the Hebrew word *shabath* which means "to cause to fail, to repose, suffer to be lacking, to put down, take away."

As we praise the Lord, we cause the enemy to fail. As we lift our voices to God, we defeat the power of Satan that would bring us into bondage. As we enter into worship, we begin to take back what the enemy has stolen from us.

When you understand this, spiritual warfare is no longer drudgery. That's why Paul could say, "Fight the good fight of faith" (1 Tim. 6:12). It's a good fight when you know your enemy is fleeing in terror.

God wants to give us a new mentality regarding the devil and his works. He has been thought of as being the big, bad wolf, and we, the body of Christ, are the three little pigs. Our perception of spiritual warfare is as follows:

> Knocking at the door, Big Bad Wolf says, "Little pig, little pig, let me in!"
>
> "Not by the hair of my chinny chin chin. I resist you in Jesus' name!" replies the little Christian pig.
>
> "Then I'll huff and I'll puff and I'll blow your house down," says Big Bad Wolf.
>
> And the little pig's house is blown down because it was built out of the wood, hay and stubble of improper understanding.
>
> Being a good born-again, Spirit-filled, little pig, he runs crying to Pastor Pig, wanting him to pray for him.

This has been the church's mentality in the past concerning the devil, but now it's time to rewrite the story. I believe the present version would go something like this:

> Big Bad Wolf comes knocking at the door demanding to be let in. Now this little pig, realizing Big Bad Wolf has no right to be at his house, prepares his double-barrelled weapon of warfare with a load of the high praises of God.
>
> He returns to the front door to greet Big Bad Wolf with his weapon in hand. As he unloads both barrels on Big Bad Wolf, he proclaims to the neighbors, "Wolf hunting season is now open!" The force of revelation-knowledge from the firing of the gun defeats the threat and secures his house.

I only use this story as an analogy to illuminate the change that must come to the church's mentality. Instead of seeing the devil as a threat, I believe we need to see ourselves as a threat to his kingdom or the object of his fear.

We are not running from our enemy; instead we have him on the run. We are not in a defensive position waiting for him to attack. Rather we take the offensive and go after his kingdom aggressively. We are God's commandoes who go in behind the lines rescuing those that are held captive. We use spiritual weapons of war to blow up his communications facilities and destroy his MO (method of operation).

Praise and worship play an important role in all of this because God has ordained our praise to silence him. Again, in Psalm 8:2, the psalmist declares that it is out of the mouth of babes that God has ordained praise.

Does that mean praise is reserved for children only? Not at all. Jesus said, "Unless you...become like little children you will never enter the kingdom of heaven" (Matt. 18:3, NIV). He said to "suffer little children...to come unto me: for of such is the kingdom of heaven" (Matt. 19:14). Jesus exhorted us to be like children. Likewise, the psalmist is saying in Psalm 8 that if we praise and worship the Lord like children, He has ordained that type of praise to silence and still the enemy.

When children praise the Lord, they are uninhibited. Their expressions of praise are as natural as breathing. I have three children, Joshua, Kayla and Micah. When they were toddlers and heard music, they would move, sway and dance to it. It was a natural response.

It should be just as natural to us as children of God to dance and celebrate before the Lord when we hear music and songs of praise. But sadly we have become religiously "brain-dirtied" over a process of time. The only solution is to wash our minds with the Word of God (see Eph. 5:26). We will then begin to worship in spirit and in truth as we behold what the Bible has to say about praise and worship.

It is time for the church to arise in this hour and praise the Lord with all its might. We must become uninhibited in our praise, even as children are. Then our weapon of warfare — praise — will be unleashed on the powers of darkness and result in their demise and destruction.

THREE

EXECUTING JUDGMENTS

*Let the high praises of God
be in their mouth,
and a two-edged sword in their hand;
to execute vengeance upon the heathen,
and punishments upon the people;
to bind their kings with chains,
and their nobles with fetters of iron;
to execute upon them the judgment written:
this honor have all his saints.
Praise ye the Lord.
Psalm 149:6-9*

This particular passage of Scripture has always been one of my favorites. The part that praise plays in spiritual warfare is evident as you read it. With high praises and the Word of God (a two-edged sword) we have the ability to execute God's vengeance, inflict punishment, bind kings, bind nobles and execute judgments.

In spiritual warfare, our enemy is not people. As

noted earlier, Paul said that *"we wrestle not against flesh and blood,* but against principalities, against powers, against the rulers of the darkness of this world, against spiritual wickedness in high places" (Eph. 6:12, emphasis added). We must always keep in mind who our enemy is: the devil. Our problem is not people, but the spiritual forces that are motivating them. That realization will keep us focused on the mission God has given us to destroy the works of the devil.

Further, Paul said that "the weapons of our warfare are not carnal, but mighty through God to the pulling down of strong holds" (2 Cor. 10:9). You cannot fight a spiritual enemy with natural weapons. We must use spiritual weapons of war to combat our spiritual enemy. Praise is one of those weapons. It is a spiritual weapon of war that binds and breaks the powers of darkness.

As stated before, our praises can execute God's vengeance. God does take vengeance, for He said, "Vengeance is mine" (Rom. 12:19). God wants to settle the score in all matters and give just recompense to whom it is due. The primary target of that vengeance is the devil.

Next, in Psalm 149:8, we see that our praise will "bind kings with chains and nobles with fetters of iron." Let's first understand who the kings and nobles are that the psalmist is talking about. I believe them to be the principalities and rulers of darkness. They are the wicked demonic kings that have set up rulership and dominion in geographical locations and in people's lives. The Bible says that our praise binds them with chains and fetters of iron. As we praise the Lord, we immobilize them. We cause them to desist and stop whatever maneu-

25

vers, plans or strategies they are attempting to carry out.

The last thing that this passage reveals about our praise is that it "execute(s) the judgment written." The New International Version states it this way: "to carry out the sentence written against them."

To understand what is being said, visualize a court scene. There are many participants in court: judge, jury, defendant, plaintiff, bailiff and witnesses, along with the lawyers who represent the accused and the accuser. All of them play an important role in the outcome of a trial. After the lawyers have presented their cases before the judge and jury, the jury will go out for deliberation. After deciding whether the accused is innocent or guilty, they will return with a verdict. The verdict will then be read out loud. If found guilty, the convicted criminal will have to stand before the judge for sentencing.

Now let's suppose that someone has just been tried for armed robbery. After hearing testimony and seeing evidence, the jury decides the defendant is guilty. He stands before the judge to be sentenced. The judge pronounces a judgment or sentence upon him, saying, "I sentence you to twenty years in the state penitentiary." It would be wonderful if that alone took care of the punishment, but it doesn't. The bailiff — a courtroom police official — handcuffs the convicted criminal, puts him in a police vehicle and takes him to the penitentiary where he is incarcerated and begins to serve his term.

This act by the bailiff is the execution of the judgment that is written. The judgment or sentence by itself will not do the job. Someone must see to it that the judgment is executed or carried out.

What if in that same courtroom there was no bailiff? Do you think the convicted criminal would voluntarily check himself into the penitentiary as someone would into a hotel? Could you envision him arriving at the front gate saying, "I have a reservation for the next twenty years"? No, without a bailiff, the convicted criminal is going to run out of that courtroom, never to be seen again.

Spiritually speaking, a judgment and a sentence have been pronounced on the devil. The Word of God declares that Satan and his works are beneath our feet (Rom. 16:20). It declares that all his power has been spoiled. But this is just the pronouncing of the sentence. That sentence, or judgment, must still be executed.

We, the church, are the bailiffs in God's great courtroom, the earth, where He sits as judge. With our praise we bind the devil just as a police official would handcuff a criminal. With our praise we incarcerate him. The praises of God have divine power to execute the judgment He has declared on the enemy.

The devil is a convicted criminal, and God has a warrant out for his arrest. What are we going to do about it? Let us as the church of God arise with praise in our mouths, as we execute His judgment upon the powers of hell.

At the end of Psalm 149 we read, "This honor have all his saints" (v. 9). What honor is the psalmist talking about? The honor of executing God's judgment and vengeance on the powers of the air. Warfare praise is not a toilsome thing. It is an honor that God has bestowed upon you and me. It is done with joy in our hearts as we celebrate the victory of our Lord.

I once wondered why God didn't cast the devil into hell immediately after his rebellion. His punishment was rather to be confined to the earth to be punished by the church. We now have the honor of binding him. We have the honor of executing God's judgment and destroying Satan's kingdom.

Knowing this can change the way we view what the devil tries to throw across our paths. When we are confronted by the enemy, we have the privilege one more time of showing the devil who we are in Christ and who he is not. We then lift up our hands, raise our voices in song and dance before the Lord as we acknowledge Him as the mighty man of war who is mighty in battle through us!

FOUR

BEAT YOUR PLOWSHARES INTO SWORDS

Proclaim this among the nations:
Prepare for war!
Rouse the warriors!
Let all the fighting men
draw near and attack.
Beat your plowshares into swords
and your pruning hooks into spears.
Let the weakling say, "I am strong!"
Joel 3:9-10, NIV

Joel gives a good picture here of the army of the Lord in the last days. God is instructing us to prepare for war and to rouse the warriors, and then He tells how: "Beat your plowshares into swords." There is an important revelation in this verse that the body of Christ needs to hear. Let's not miss it.

The prophet Hosea declares, "Judah shall plow"

(10:11). The name *Judah* means "praise." Thus, the prophet is saying, "Praise shall plow."

At some time you might have heard this statement in church: "Let's praise the Lord and prepare our hearts to receive the Word of God." I used to get a little upset about that phrase because it seemed to de-emphasize worship. But that is a very scriptural statement. As we praise the Lord, we plow and prepare our hearts to receive the incorruptible seed, the Word of God. Any farmer knows that before he plants seed he must first prepare the soil by plowing. Before we can plant the incorruptible seed of the Word of God, we must first plow the ground, our hearts, in which it is to be planted.

Praise and worship act as that plow. That's one of the reasons they come before the teaching and preaching of the Word rather than after it. Seed has a greater opportunity of bearing fruit if it's planted in plowed soil. Again, Judah (praise) shall plow.

But then notice what the prophet Joel says about your plow: "Beat your plow into a sword." I believe the Spirit of God is saying, "Make your praise a weapon of war." How do we do this? Revelation-knowledge is the hammer we use to beat our plows into swords, to make praise a weapon of war.

It is rare that any spiritual experience can be entered into without a revelation for appropriating it. Hearing the Word brought revelation for appropriating our salvation. Hearing the Word also brought revelation for appropriating the infilling of the Holy Spirit. Likewise, to be able to use praise as a weapon of war, we must first have a revelation that God has ordained our praise for such a purpose.

There is a difference between celebration and having a revelation of your celebration. Praise and celebration without a revelation of its power have little effect in the realm of the spirit.

Let me give you an example. We could take a drunk man off the street and bring him into church. This man could say the sinner's prayer simply by repeating what he was told. But if there was not first a revelation of the lordship of Jesus and the fact that God raised Jesus from the dead, that man would go away just as unsaved as he was before he said the sinner's prayer. Why? Because he said words without understanding and revelation.

Unfortunately, much of the church is like that. We come to church and praise the Lord with no understanding and revelation of the power God has put in our praise. Consequently, nothing happens.

The solution is to receive a revelation of what the Bible has to say about praise and worship, particularly in its application as a weapon of war. Then when we come together to praise and worship the Lord, there will be a release of power. We will then affect the spirit realm.

> I will gather all nations, and will bring
> them down into the valley of Jehoshaphat,
> and will plead with them there for my peo-
> ple and for my heritage Israel (Joel 3:2).

This verse has great significance to us as the inheritance and the people of the Lord. Jehoshaphat's enemies were defeated by the praises of God in the valley of Jehoshaphat. (A later chapter will deal with this in more depth.) This account is found in 2 Chronicles 20. When faced with insurmountable odds, Jehoshaphat appointed singers and musicians to go out at the head of the army to praise the Lord. As they praised the Lord, God brought confusion in the camp of the enemy, and they rose up and destroyed one another. So we could say that the valley of Jehoshaphat is the place where *praise ascends.*

This sheds new light on this Scripture verse. Where does God enter into judgment? The valley of Jehoshaphat, the place where praise ascends. Where are God's judgments executed? The valley of Jehoshaphat, the place where praise ascends. God's judgments are executed on our enemy, the devil, when praise ascends, just as in the day of Jehoshaphat.

The Word of God declares that all the things that were written in the Old Testament were written for our example. The story of Jehoshaphat was not penned by the Spirit of God so that we would have another good Bible story to tell our children. Rather it was written so we could be "followers of them who through faith and patience inherit the promises" (Heb. 6:12). This was written so that we can see with our physical eyes what our praise does in the spirit realm.

Another verse in Joel 3 reiterates the same thing.

> Let the nations be roused; let them advance into the Valley of Jehoshaphat, for there I will sit to judge all the nations on every side (v. 12, NIV).

I believe the Spirit is calling the church in this hour to become a radical, militant people who are warriors in the Spirit. Don't use the old excuse, "Well, you know, that's just not my personality." Being a warrior has nothing to do with your personality. It has to do with the family you belong to. If you are born of God you are a warrior because His seed is in you and He is a warrior. Hallelujah! You have been drafted into the army of the Lord. Don't go AWOL. Get in the fight as God leads us into victorious battle.

> Beat your plowshares into swords and your pruning hooks into spears. Let the weakling say, "I am strong!" (Joel 3:10, NIV).

We sing several songs that contain this phrase: "Let the weak say, 'I am strong.' " The location of this verse is very interesting. In the context of Scripture, it refers to people who are getting themselves ready to go to war. It is an exhortation for those who feel too weak to go out and fight to rouse themselves by declaring that they are strong! This was a Scripture passage given for warriors.

As a matter of fact, the word translated *strong* is the Hebrew word *gibbor*. It means "warrior" or "tyrant." The verse actually says, "Let the weak say, 'I am a warrior.' " The Spirit of God is prophetically telling the body of Christ to declare, "We are warriors."

I like that word *tyrant*. A tyrant strips all rights and privileges from his subjects. We need to be tyrants in the spirit! We shouldn't give the devil an inch. Rather we need to strip all rights and privileges from him that he has stolen from us. It is time for us to take our stand in the spirit.

To some people, speech like this may sound as if I am a mean person. But my natural personality is not that of a fighter. I was in only a few fights in all of my school years. They were very short — the guy hit me, and I hit the ground. The fight was over. But what I am saying is that we must become violent when it comes to fighting devils. Jesus said, "The violent take it by force" (Matt. 11:12).

Before we leave the subject of beating your plowshares into swords, let me share the "flip side" of this. Micah 4:3 states:

> He will judge between many peoples and will settle disputes for strong nations far and wide. They will beat their swords into plowshares and their spears into pruning hooks. Nation will not take up sword against nation, nor will they train for war anymore (NIV).

This appears to contradict Joel 3:10, but actually it does not. Let me share some different points about this passage for your consideration.

- *The church, for the most part, has never beat its plow into a sword.* We will not beat our swords into plows until we first beat our plows into swords. A day will come after all our enemies are defeated and crushed when we will beat our swords into plows. But all our enemies have not yet been subdued. There are still giants that must be slain. Until all our enemies are subdued, we must use our swords. A warrior doesn't lay his weapon down until his enemy is slain.

- *This Scripture passage pertains to God's settling disputes between nations.* God is not going to act as a peacemaker between us and the devil. As a matter of fact, Jesus said, "Occupy till I come" (Luke 19:13). *Occupy* is a military term that literally means "to take possession of." I believe this term can be paraphrased to say, "Run the devil out of town and subdue what I have given to you until I come." Our attitude with the devil is to be "show no mercy and take no prisoners."

- *We don't beat our swords into plows until after all of God's judgments have been executed.* A day is coming when there will be peace on earth, and we will not train for war anymore. But that day is not here yet. During the millennial reign, we will rule and reign with Jesus here on earth for a thousand years. There will be peace as the kingdom of God is finalized. Our enemy, the devil, will be locked up in hell. But until then we must take up our weapons of war and blast him off the earth.

I believe the Spirit of God is crying for the church to arise in strength and maturity. It is time for us to run to the battle with our weapons of war without looking back. We must be like Gideon's army. The Bible says they were "faint, yet pursuing" (Judg. 8:4). When you begin to feel faint, take a dose of the Word of God. "Let the weak say, 'I am strong.'" Rouse yourself and take up your sword and wield it against your enemy. Let your praise become a weapon of war as you lift your voice to Him!

FIVE

MIGHTY MAN
OF WAR

The Lord is a warrior; the Lord is his name.
Pharaoh's chariots and his army
he has hurled into the sea.
Exodus 15:3-4, NIV

The Lord will march out like a mighty man,
like a warrior he will stir up His zeal;
with a shout he will raise the battle cry
and will triumph over his enemies.
Isaiah 42:13, NIV

I saw heaven standing open
and there before me was a white horse,
whose rider is called Faithful and True.
With justice he judges and makes war.
Revelation 19:11, NIV

The Bible reveals that part of God's character is that of a warrior. Both the Old and New Testaments testify of this. As members of the body of Christ and to engage successfully in spiritual war, we need to have this revelation of God's character.

Paul told the Ephesians to be "imitators of God" (Eph. 5:1, NIV). And to be imitators of God, we must have a revelation of His whole character. Not only is He a God of love, peace and joy, but He is also a warrior. Paul said, "Behold therefore the goodness and severity of God" (Rom. 11:22). Paul is saying we can see the whole character of God by looking at the whole counsel of the Word of God.

If we emphasize one aspect of the character of God, then we get a distorted picture of who God is. For the past couple of decades a great deal of teaching has come forth on the goodness and love of God. I thank God for all we have learned. But it seems as if we have had little teaching on some of the other attributes of His character. One of those is the attribute of warrior.

Why is it important to teach this attribute? First, what you reach in God will be in direct proportion to your revelation of Him. Someone who does not have a revelation of Jesus as Savior cannot receive Him as Savior. Someone who does not have a revelation of Jesus as healer, Jehovah-Rapha, will not get healed. Likewise, without a revelation of Jesus as warrior, the Lord of hosts, we will not be able to wage successful, spiritual warfare. God moves on our behalf according to our faith and knowledge of Him.

A second reason for teaching on this attribute of God's character is so we will know in what atmosphere the Lord manifests Himself as a warrior. This is where praise and worship enter the picture. As we study the following Scripture portions, we will see that Jesus arises as a mighty man of war in the midst of praise and worship. Something about praise stirs the heart of God. As we praise, He rises up with a zeal and vengeance against our enemies.

> Sing to the Lord a new song, his praise from the ends of the earth, you who go down to the sea, and all that is in it, you islands, and all who live in them. Let the desert and its towns raise their voices; let the settlements where Kedar lives rejoice. Let the people of Sela sing for joy; let them shout from the mountaintops. Let them give glory to the Lord and proclaim His praise in the islands (Is. 42:10-12, NIV).

Here we see an exhortation for people to praise the Lord. By the Spirit of God, Isaiah instructs them to raise their voices, rejoice, sing a new song, shout, sing for joy, give glory to God and proclaim His praise. The next verse tells us what happens when people express their praise to the Lord:

> The Lord will march out like a mighty man, like a warrior he will stir up his zeal; with a shout he will raise the battle cry and will triumph over his enemies (Is. 42:13, NIV).

What happens when we praise the Lord? The Lord marches out against our enemies. As we lift our voices to the Lord with shouts of joy, His zeal is stirred. As we glorify God with heart, soul and strength (spirit, soul and body), the battle cry arises, and He triumphs over our enemies.

The original Hebrew language contained no punctuation marks. All punctuation has been placed there by the translators. Without changing the words, I would like to take the liberty of changing a few punctuation marks. I believe this will

39

enable us to see this verse in a different light.

> The Lord will march out like a mighty man, like a warrior. He will stir up his zeal with a SHOUT! He will raise the battle cry and will triumph over his enemies.

What is revealed to us is that the zeal within the heart of God is stirred with shouting of praises. We could even read it like this: The Lord will march out like a mighty man, like a warrior. His zeal will be stirred with shouts of praise.

To substantiate this as a scriptural principle, here are some other Scripture passages that say essentially the same thing:

> O clap your hands, all ye people; shout unto God with the voice of triumph. God is gone up [ascended] with a shout (Ps. 47:1,5).

> God has ascended amid shouts of joy (Ps. 47:5, NIV).

> Every stroke the Lord lays on them [the enemy] with his punishing rod will be to the music of tambourines and harps, as he fights them in battle with the blows of his arm (Is. 30:32, NIV).

The emphasis is on the connection between our praise and God's battle with our enemy. As we rejoice and shout, God arises in our midst and scatters our enemies.

> May God arise, may his enemies be scattered; may his foes flee before him (Ps. 68:1, NIV).

When God arises, His enemies are always scattered. The devil is no match for almighty God and His church. The key is having Him arise in our midst.

So how does He arise? Psalm 47:5 says He arises amid shouts of joy. Isaiah 42:13 declares that His zeal is stirred with a shout, and in the midst of that He raises the battle cry, triumphing over His (and our) enemies. Isaiah 30:32 says that every stroke the Lord lays on our enemy is done "to the music of tambourines and harps" as He fights them with the blows of His arm. That's the reason the psalmist could say:

> His right hand, and his holy arm, hath gotten him the victory (Ps. 98:1).

The psalmist had a revelation that God would fight on our behalf as we praised His name. He had a revelation of the Lord as the mighty man of war. He knew that the Lord would march out on our behalf if we would shout His praise in faith.

The psalmist David was "a man after [God's] own heart" (1 Sam. 13:14, NIV). I used to think it was because David was a lover of God. After further study of David's life, I do not believe that was the only reason he was referred to as "a man after God's own heart."

David was a man who had a reputation in the kingdom of Israel. Saul asked his servant to find someone to play the harp before him. Let's observe what the servant ascribed to David (1 Sam. 16:18): He knows how to play the harp. He is brave. He is a warrior. He speaks well. He is fine-looking. The Lord is with him.

Knowing how to play a harp and speak well and being fine-looking would not make you a man after God's heart. But notice what the testimony about David also said. He was *brave*, and he was a *warrior*.

Nobody else in Israel was jumping at the chance to face Goliath, except David, the *warrior — the man after God's own heart*. No one else in Israel was willing to risk his life to fight a lion and a bear for a sheep, except David, the *warrior — the man after God's own heart*. When Saul told David that he could marry his daughter if he brought Saul one hundred Philistine foreskins (1 Sam. 18:25), David slew enough Philistines to double the requirement: David, the *warrior — the man after God's own heart*.

Yes, David was a worshipper and a lover of God, but he was equally a warrior, a man of war. David knew his God and did everything within his power to be like Him.

David was a warrior, but there was one who was an even greater warrior than David. His name was Jesus. He warred against sin, sickness, religious traditions of men, hypocrisy and many other things. In Matthew 21 we can see one of the greatest demonstrations of this aspect of God's character: Jesus' triumphal entry into Jerusalem on the back of a donkey.

> Say to the Daughter of Zion,
>   See, your king comes to you,

> gentle and riding on a donkey,
> on a colt, the foal of a donkey....

A very large crowd spread their cloaks on the road, while others cut branches from the trees and spread them on the road. The crowds that went ahead of him and those that followed shouted,

> "Hosanna to the Son of David!"
> "Blessed is he who comes in the
> name of the Lord!"
> "Hosanna in the highest!"

When Jesus entered Jerusalem, the whole city was stirred and asked, "Who is this?" The crowds answered, "This is Jesus, the prophet from Nazareth in Galilee" (vv. 5,8-11, NIV).

Let's examine what was happening. Meek and gentle Jesus was riding into Jerusalem on a donkey. On His way to the temple a large crowd began to have an outdoor praise celebration in honor of Him. Many were taking off their cloaks and laying them in the road for Jesus to pass over. Others were cutting down branches from trees and laying them in the road. All of them were shouting praises so loudly that the "whole city was stirred."

When Jesus arrived at the temple, something happened:

> Jesus entered the temple area and drove out all who were buying and selling there. He overturned the tables of the money

changers and the benches of those selling doves. "It is written," he said to them, "'My house will be called a house of prayer, but you are making it a den of robbers'" (vv. 12-13, NIV).

The blind and the lame came to him at the temple, and he healed them. But when the chief priests and the teachers of the law saw the wonderful things he did and the children shouting in the temple area, "Hosanna to the Son of David," they were indignant. "Do you hear what these children are saying?" they asked him. "Yes," replied Jesus, "have you never read,

'From the lips of children and infants you have ordained praise?'" (vv. 14-16, NIV).

I want you to see what motivated Jesus to go into the temple and drive the money changers out. I do not believe it was merely the activities of the money changers, because Jesus had seen them before at the temple. It was not the selling of the doves, for this had been going on for years, and Jesus had never done anything about it.

What caused Jesus to arise with righteous indignation in a violent assault against these men? *It was the shouts of praise that were coming from the people.*

When Jesus first entered Jerusalem, He was meek and gentle. But as He rode through town toward the temple, there was a metamorphosis. As the shouts of praise were lifted to Him, His zeal was stirred just as Isaiah 42:13 declared. At no other time in the history of His walk on earth had there been such an open demonstration of praise, worship and celebration in honor of Him. The Lord was getting ready to "march out like a mighty man" as He heard the praises of the people.

Upon arriving at the temple, having been stirred by the shouts of praise, He made a whip out of some cords (His punishing rod) and proceeded to drive out the money changers. He then began to overturn the tables of the dove salesmen.

In chapter 1 of this book we saw that God is restoring the tabernacle of David for a purpose. That purpose is to possess. We learned that the word *possess* means to drive out the previous tenants. "Jesus entered the temple area and *drove out* all who were buying and selling there" (Matt. 21:12, NIV). In the midst of a praise celebration Jesus drove out the previous tenants (the money changers) and then declared, "My house will be called a house of prayer." In essence He was saying, "This is My house, and you can't have it!" He possessed what was rightfully His.

Verses 15 and 16 of Matthew 21 reveal an interesting event. The chief priests and teachers of the Law, the religious leaders of the day, were indignant when they heard the children shouting praises to the Lord. Demonstrative praise and worship always upset religious spirits. Demons of pride hate shouting and dancing because it is not "dignified."

Those in leadership in the body of Christ today must not mimic the response from the religious leaders of Jesus' day. They did not get upset with Jesus about the miracles He did that day or the fact that He had just caused a big ruckus in the temple. They got upset because people were *praising demonstratively!* They tried to get Jesus to tell the people to stop.

But Jesus told them, "If these should hold their peace, the stones would immediately cry out" (Luke 19:40). In other words, "you cannot stop the praises that belong to Me."

The people who were throwing their cloaks in the road and cutting down branches were never accused by Jesus of being "in the flesh." There is no place in the Bible where it says to take off your coat and throw it in the road in praise to the Lord. Neither is there any place where it says to cut down branches and throw them in the road in praise to the Lord. Yet the people did that, and Jesus never rebuked them. As a matter of fact, you cannot find anywhere in the Bible where Jesus ever rebuked people for praising and worshipping God. He encouraged and defended the ones who did.

A lesson can be learned from this. Anything you can do to glorify God, as long as it does not go contrary to Scripture, do it! If you can glorify God with a laser light show, then do it! If God can be glorified through dance presentations, then do them! He is not opposed to our using creativity in our worship expression.

The only people who discouraged and condemned demonstrative worship were religious leaders. As these teachers of the Law heard the children praising Jesus, they asked Him: "Do you hear what these children are saying?" (Matt. 21:16, NIV).

Jesus began His reply by saying, "Yes, have you never read...?" Let me point out here that it would do many people good to read what the Bible teaches about worship. Jesus went on to say, " 'From the lips of children and infants you have ordained praise.' " Of all the passages on praise that Jesus could have quoted, He chose Psalm 8:2.

> From the lips of children and infants
> you have ordained praise
> because of your enemies,
> to silence the foe and the avenger (NIV).

Note how the verse concludes: "Because of your enemies, to silence the foe and the avenger." Jesus was defending the children's praises, but He was explaining everything that had just happened in the temple area. He was saying, "This is why I came into the temple and drove out the money changers. This is why I overturned the tables of the dove salesmen. God has ordained praise like that from these children because it causes Me to rise up against My enemies (the money changers) and put them to silence." Hallelujah!

We have heard it said, "If Jesus healed then, He is still healing today. If Jesus delivered then, He is still delivering today." These statements are true. But let me propose this to you. If in the midst of demonstrative praise Jesus arose as a man of war then, He is still arising today. He is the same yesterday, today and forever. Our God is a warrior!

SIX

IN THE PRESENCE OF THE LORD OF HOSTS

But thou art holy,
O thou that inhabitest the praises of Israel.
Psalm 22:3

The Lord is my strength and song, and he is become
my salvation: he is my God, and I will prepare him
an habitation; my father's God, and I will exalt him.
The Lord is a man of war: the Lord is his name.
Exodus 15:2-3

I will praise thee, O Lord, with my whole heart; I will
show forth all thy marvellous works. I will be glad
and rejoice in thee: I will sing praise to thy name,
O thou most High. When mine enemies are turned
back, they shall fall and perish at thy presence.
Psalm 9:1-3

Most Christians have probably heard at one time or another that God inhabits the praises of His people. Before a worship service begins, a pastor will often exhort the congregation: "Let us come this morning and allow the presence of God to be manifested as we praise Him. The Word of God declares that God inhabits the praises of His people. Allow the Lord to inhabit your praise as lift your voice in song to Him."

But lack of knowledge or religious "mind-sets" have hindered us from understanding the nature and work of God who inhabits our praise.

For most Christians the only revelation of God's character is that of a loving, merciful Savior. Thank God we have that revelation. If it were not for the love and mercy of God, we would all be lost and without hope. But God's character is more than just love, grace and mercy, as wonderful as those attributes are.

We learned in the previous chapter that our God is a man of war. He is a warrior. The Bible also refers to God as the Lord of hosts. The word *hosts* is the Hebrew word *tsaba*. This word means "a mass of persons organized for war." So when the Bible refers to the Lord as the Lord of hosts, it is referring to the Lord of armies or the Lord of people organized for war. As a matter of fact, the Bible refers to God as the Lord of hosts in 244 places. This is five times more than any other descriptive or redemptive name ascribed to Him.

In the New Testament God is referred to twice as Lord of Sabaoth. The word *sabaoth* is the transliteration of the Hebrew word *tsaba* meaning "armies." Strong's concordance defines this Greek word as "a military epithet of God." God wants us to know that He is Lord of a fighting and warring people.

After the children of Israel crossed the Red Sea, God displayed His mighty power in the destruction of the Egyptian army.

> And the Lord said unto Moses, Stretch out thine hand over the sea, that the waters

> may come again upon the Egyptians, upon their chariots, and upon their horsemen. And Moses stretched forth his hand over the sea, and the sea returned to his strength when the morning appeared; and the Egyptians fled against it; and the Lord overthrew the Egyptians in the midst of the sea. And the waters returned, and covered the chariots, and the horsemen, and all the host of Pharaoh that came into the sea after them...and Israel saw the Egyptians dead upon the sea shore (Ex. 14:26-28,30).

God spoke to Moses to stretch out his hand over the sea so that the Egyptians would be drowned. The waters collapsed on the Egyptians, and they were totally annihilated. The Israelites saw dead bodies scattered along the seashore. At this sight Moses told them to strike up the band.

> Then sang Moses and the children of Israel this song unto the Lord, and spake saying, I will sing unto the Lord for he hath triumphed gloriously: the horse and the rider hath he [God] thrown into the sea (Ex. 15:1).

On seeing the enemy destroyed, Moses decided it was time to celebrate. They began to sing a song of praise to the Lord, most likely in an antiphonal manner. (An antiphonal song is carried out in responsive, alternating parts. Usually the worship leader sings a short phrase, and the congregation then echoes it.) They rejoiced and danced for the mighty victory that had just been wrought. In fact, they praised the Lord for killing the Egyptian army.

Visualize this for a moment: The Israelites had just crossed the Red Sea, and now there were dead Egyptian bodies lying on the shore. As the Israelites sing, Miriam the prophetess takes a tambourine and begins to lead all the women in dance there on the seashore. They were rejoicing in song because the judgment of God had been executed upon their enemies.

Many of us have sung "The Horse and the Rider" as a nice, joyful, praise song that is fun to sing. But actually we are praising the Lord for destroying — killing — the Egyptian army.

As Moses and the children of Israel were celebrating, they sang, "I will prepare him an habitation" (Ex. 15:2). How do we prepare a habitation for God? Psalm 22:3 says that God inhabits the praises of His people. We prepare a habitation for God with our praise. Our praise creates a place where God can dwell and manifest His presence.

The Bible tells us that God inhabits or is enthroned in three places: in heaven, in our hearts as believers and in our praise.

We want to concentrate on the third — God being enthroned in our praise. Knowing that God inhabits our praises, we then proceed to find out the character and nature of Him for whom we are preparing a habitation. We have already established that the Lord is a warrior and that He is the Lord of hosts. Our God is militant. Our praise prepares a habitation for the mighty warrior, the Lord of hosts. Moses had a revelation of this. Immediately after saying, "I will prepare him an habitation," he said, "the Lord is a man of war: the Lord is his name" (Ex. 15:3).

The manifest presence of God is the tangible (sensed or felt) manifestation of God's character and nature. At one time or another, all of us have probably sensed His presence in our lives.

Since God's character and nature are multifaceted, so is the presence of God. When you sense the peace of God in a worship service, you are sensing a manifestation of Jehovah-Shalom. If you sense a healing anointing, God is manifesting Himself as Jehovah-Rapha, the Lord our Healer. These more familiar manifestations of the presence of God may have been the extent of our revelation of God's character and nature. God responds to us in accordance to our faith.

Jesus said, "According to your faith be it unto you" (Matt. 9:29). We have had limited faith to receive the presence of God except as love, peace, joy, healing and deliverance. God's presence will be manifested according to our revelation of His character and nature.

The Spirit of God is saying to the church in this hour: "I will not stay in the box you have built for Me with limited revelation of who I am. I am bringing revelation of My character and nature that will allow Me to flow freely as I desire to manifest My presence with might and great power. I want to manifest My presence as the mighty man of war, the lion of Judah and Lord Sabaoth; the Lord of hosts who is mighty in battle."

God has a purpose for His manifest presence. First of all, God desires to minister *to* us with His presence. The Bible says, "In thy presence is fulness of joy" (Ps. 16:11). We are to be a joyful people.

Second, God desires to minister *through* us with His presence. When God manifests His presence as Jehovah-Rapha, we should pray for others to receive their healing. I equate this to the story of the angel who troubled the waters at the pool of Bethesda. Whoever stepped in first was healed (John 5:4). When God's presence is manifested in a healing anointing it is easier to get people healed. At that time, as colaborers with God, we need to step out and minister to one another.

Finally, God wants to destroy our enemies with His presence. God's presence is manifested for the purpose of spiritual warfare. Psalm 68:2 says, "Let the wicked perish at the presence of God." David said in Psalm 9:3, "When mine enemies are turned back, they shall fall and perish at thy presence." God doesn't manifest His presence just to thrill us. He has objectives to accomplish.

As Moses declared, we prepare a habitation for the Lord who is a man of war. If we prepare a habitation for the Lord who is a man of war, then God desires to show Himself to us in that manner. A man of war fights. Our praise prepares a habitation for the Lord to manifest Himself as the mighty man of war and rise up and fight against our enemies.

We are colaborers with God, working together with the Lord. When we sense the presence of Lord Sabaoth, the Lord of hosts, the Lord is actually sounding the battle cry for His army to follow Him into battle.

We may sense a "spirit of warfare." This is when God's Spirit prompts us to enter with our weapons of praise into spiritual warfare against the spirits of darkness. *This is the presence of God.*

As you read the story of David meeting Goliath, you can see that David had a revelation of the Lord of hosts. After the giant threatened him, he declared prophetically the fate of Goliath.

> Thou comest to me with a sword, and with a spear, and with a shield: but I come to thee in the name of the Lord of hosts, the God of the armies of Israel, whom thou hast defied (1 Sam. 17:45).

David was saying, "It is not my sling and stone that will kill you, but it is my God, the Lord of hosts, who will serve as my weapon." Goliath came against David with natural weapons, but David was armed with the revelation that the God he served was the Lord of hosts. It was David's trust in that revelation that caused his sling and stone to be empowered by God.

Likewise, that revelation of the God who inhabits our praises will give power to our praises. We will be able to say with David, "[My enemies] shall fall and perish at thy presence" (Ps. 9:3).

God's presence is not manifested to give us a spiritually euphoric experience. We must know that the One who inhabits our praises is almighty God, the mighty warrior, the Lord of hosts. Not only is there fullness of joy in His presence, but there is also complete victory, as the Lord Sabaoth leads us into battle, and His enemies perish at His presence.

SEVEN

THE POWER OF THE SHOUT

*Clap your hands, all you nations; shout to God
with cries of joy...God has ascended amid shouts
of joy, the Lord amid the sounding of trumpets.*
Psalm 47:1,5, NIV

*Let God arise, let his enemies be scattered: let them
also that hate him flee before him. As smoke is driven
away, so drive them away: as wax melteth before the
fire, so let the wicked perish at the presence of God.*
Psalm 68:1-2

*The Lord will march out like a mighty man,
like a warrior he will stir up his zeal,
with a shout he will raise the battle cry
and will triumph over his enemies.*
Isaiah 42:13, NIV

There are many different ways the Bible tells us
to express our praise to the Lord. Shouting is
one of those ways. Exactly why God desires us to
shout, I do not know. But nonetheless He has told
us to shout to Him. He has also laid out in the
Word of God spiritual principles for the shout.

To the natural mind, shouting to God seems silly.
After all, God is not hard of hearing and does not

need us to speak a little louder. But the Word of God reveals that the shout releases something in and through us. God established the shout of praise for our benefit.

The word *shout* is the Hebrew word *ruwa*. It means "to split the ears with sound; to mar especially by breaking." God has put power in shouting. When we shout, we split the devil's ears with praise. We mar and break up his kingdom. The fortresses the enemy had built begin to crumble and fall as we shout praise to the Lord.

In chapter 5 we examined the account of Jesus' triumphal entry into Jerusalem. In the midst of this praise Jesus arrived at the temple and drove out all the money changers and dove salesmen.

In the account of the triumphal entry we see a demonstration of a spiritual principle. Psalm 47:5 declares God arises amid shouting. In the King James Version we read, "God is gone up with a shout." The word *gone* is the Hebrew word *alah*. One of the definitions for this word is "stir up." So we could read that verse like this: God is stirred up against our enemies when we shout His praise.

We see this spiritual principle demonstrated in the triumphal entry of Jesus and the cleansing of the temple. Let's look at it from a little different angle. Psalm 68:1 says, "Let God arise, let His enemies be scattered." How do we let God arise? We have already established that God arises or is stirred up with shouting. The Hebrew word translated *arise* in this passage is defined as "to rise, rouse up, stir up."

We see that when God arises or is stirred up, His enemies are scattered. The word *scattered* means "to dash in pieces or break." Now let us put it all together and see what's actually being said:

> God is stirred up against our enemies with shouts of praise. As He is stirred up, or arises, His enemies are dashed into pieces, and their kingdoms break and are destroyed.

This brings us back to the original definition of shout, which is "to mar by breaking."

As mentioned earlier, the accounts and stories written in both Old and New Testaments were written for our example (1 Cor. 10:11) and to demonstrate spiritual principles. Let's look at some that demonstrate the principle of the shout. One of the most familiar accounts is that of Joshua at Jericho, found in chapters 5 and 6 of Joshua.

> Now when Joshua was near Jericho, he looked up and saw a man standing in front of him with a drawn sword in his hand. Joshua went up to him and asked, "Are you for us or for our enemies?"
>
> "Neither," he replied, "but as commander of the army of the Lord I have now come."
>
> Then Joshua fell facedown to the ground in reverence, and asked him, "What message does my Lord have for his servant?"
>
> The commander of the Lord's army replied, "Take off your sandals, for the place where you are standing is holy." And Joshua did so (5:13-15, NIV).

Then the Lord said to Joshua, "See, I have

delivered Jericho into your hands, along with its king and its fighting men. March around the city once with all the armed men. Do this for six days. Have seven priests carry trumpets of rams' horns in front of the ark. On the seventh day, march around the city seven times, with the priests blowing the trumpets. When you hear them sound a long blast on the trumpets, have all the people give a loud shout; then the wall of the city will collapse and the people will go up, every man straight in" (6:2-5, NIV).

The story unfolds as the commander of the army of the Lord approaches Joshua. Interestingly enough, Joshua does not recognize who it is. He has never seen the Lord like this. The Lord is standing with a drawn sword. Joshua has known the Lord as deliverer, provider and sustainer but not as warrior. The Lord appears to Joshua to give him a fresh revelation of who He is so that he can carry out the mission of God.

He then receives battle instructions from the Lord — a divine strategy. The Lord instructs Joshua to march around the city of Jericho one time each day for six consecutive days. On the seventh day, they are to march around the city seven times. Then the priests are to sound a long blast on the trumpets, and the people are to "give a loud shout." At this, the walls will fall.

Joshua then instructs the people and proceeds to carry out the battle plan.

On the seventh day, they got up at daybreak and marched around the city seven times in the same manner, except that on that day they circled the city seven times. The seventh time around, when the priests sounded the trumpet blast, Joshua commanded the people, "Shout! For the Lord has given you the city!"...When the trumpets sounded, the people shouted, and at the sound of the trumpet, when the people gave a loud shout, the wall collapsed; so every man charged straight in, and they took the city (6:15-16,20, NIV).

As all the people gave a loud shout, the walls collapsed. Again, we have to ask why this story is in the Bible. Of course, one reason is because it was a historical event that actually happened. But Paul declared that these things were written for our example. So what are the principles and truths God wants to reveal to us in this story?

One is simply the blessing of obedience. But a spiritual principle governed even the practice of obedience. I believe the principle was that of the power of the shout!

Another truth is that of the necessity of a divine strategy. But then why did God use the strategy of offering up a shout? Could this be used again, or was it just an isolated incident? It was to be an example for us to follow.

God was demonstrating the mighty weapon of the shout through the Israelites. God arises amid shouts of praise, and His enemies are scattered. As Joshua and the Israelites shouted, their enemies' defense was destroyed. When we shout unto God with the voice of triumph, the defense of our enemies is destroyed, and we are able to go in and spoil his goods. We can go up and possess what rightfully belongs to the church. Hallelujah!

The account of Gideon and the Midianites demonstrates another great victory involving shouting.

> Dividing the three hundred men into three companies, he placed trumpets and empty jars in the hands of all of them, with torches inside. "Watch me," he told them. "Follow my lead. When I get to the edge of the camp, do exactly as I do. When I and all who are with me blow our trumpets, then from all around the camp blow yours and *shout*, 'For the Lord and for Gideon.'"
>
> Gideon and the hundred men with him reached the edge of the camp at the beginning of the middle watch, just after they had changed the guard. They blew their trumpets and broke the jars that were in their hands. The three companies blew the trumpets and smashed the jars. Grasping the torches in their left hands and holding in their right hands the trumpets they were to blow, they *shouted*, "A sword for the Lord and Gideon!" While each man held his position around the camp, all the Midianites ran, crying out as they fled (Judg. 7:16-21, NIV, emphasis added).

Once again we see how shouting is used in warfare. As the Midianites heard the trumpets and the shouting, they ran in terror. The Bible goes on to tell us that the men of the Midianite army turned

60

on each other and began to kill one another. Confusion was brought into the camp of the enemy through the joyful sound. As the Midianites heard the shout they scattered.

In the book of 1 Kings, we find another interesting account concerning two of David's sons. One was named Adonijah; the other was named Solomon. As King David lay dying, a question arose as to who would be king in David's place. Adonijah decided that he would take advantage of the situation and usurp the throne to be king. He gathered men around him who would agree to his plot, and he proclaimed himself as king.

Nathan the prophet, upon hearing of Adonijah's uprising, told Bathsheba, David's wife and the mother of Solomon. He instructed her to make David aware of Adonijah's rebellion. She was to remind David of his promise to make Solomon king. When David heard of Adonijah's behavior, he instructed Nathan the prophet and Zadok the priest to get Solomon and anoint him king over Israel. Then he said, "Blow the trumpet and shout, 'Long live King Solomon!'"

So Zadok the priest, Nathan the prophet, Benaiah son of Jehoiada, the Kerethites and the Pelethites went down and put Solomon on King David's mule and escorted him to Gihon. Zadok the priest took the horn of oil from the sacred tent and anointed Solomon. Then they sounded the trumpet and all the people *shouted*, "Long live King Solomon!" And all the people went up after him, playing flutes and rejoicing greatly, so that the ground shook with the sound (1 Kings 1:38-40, NIV, emphasis added).

These passages picture an inaugural celebration. All the people shouted and rejoiced until the "ground shook with the sound." Can you imagine this? The intensity of sound in the Super Dome with a capacity crowd may not have been as loud as it was on that day.

Meanwhile, Adonijah was feasting with all his friends, probably talking about the changes he would make now that he was king. While they were feasting across town, they heard the noise. Jonathan, son of Abiathar the priest, ran in to tell Adonijah and his guests the reason for the celebration. After the announcement was made,

> all Adonijah's guests rose in alarm and dispersed (1 Kings 1:49, NIV).

As a result of the people's rejoicing and shouting "Long live King Solomon," Adonijah's men were gripped with fear and scattered. Adonijah was so afraid that he took hold of the horns of the altar and would not let go until he got word that Solomon would not kill him.

As the people shouted, the usurpers were scattered. They rose in alarm and dispersed. When Satan hears the shouts of God's people proclaiming Jesus as king, he and his demonic powers flee in alarm. We terrorize the devil with shouts.

The home-field advantage in sports competition also demonstrates the principle of the shout. Playing at home gives a team an advantage because more people will cheer — shout — for the home team. These shouts can demoralize the visiting team and sap its enthusiasm, zeal and energy.

These shouts cause the home team to play more aggressively, with a greater degree of confidence. You may ask how this relates to Christians. In one sense, we are in a competition. It's Jesus and the church against Satan and his demonic powers.

We have the home-field advantage. The Bible says that the "earth is the Lord's, and the fulness thereof; the world, and they that dwell therein" (Ps. 24:1). The Lord owns the stadium in which the church competes. The devil is the visiting team. Having been kicked out of heaven, the devil is visiting earth on his way to hell.

Church members and heavenly beings fill the stadium. As they cheer and shout, someone many times greater than the best National Football League quarterback enters the playing field. Our quarterback, Jesus, calls the plays as He instructs the church in what to do. His plays are prophetic insight, revelation, activation and demonstration. The devil does not have a chance as the people in the stadium shout praises and cheer for Jesus.

I use this analogy only to help you understand what power God has invested in the shout. We are not trying to compare Jesus with famous earthly quarterbacks. There is no comparison. These analogies deepen our understanding of the principles God has ordained in His Word.

A fellow minister related a story of an exercise he participated in while in the U.S. Air Force. The exercise involved hand-to-hand combat with pugil sticks. During the exercise his opponent struck him with a forceful blow to the abdomen, knocking the breath out of him. He then fought back, land-ing several good blows.

At that point, his comrades began to shout and cheer at a deafening level. The shouts stimulated the rush of extra adrenaline and strength, resulting in the defeat of his opponent.

Once again a shout stirred up zeal. This is a spiritual principle that God has put into operation, and it applies even in natural things.

Several years ago I was leading worship in a church that was holding a prophetic conference. Little did I know that God was going to teach me firsthand the power of the shout.

The conference began on a Tuesday evening and ended on Sunday evening. I sensed one of the most oppressive atmospheres I had ever been in as we began the conference. I was tired from a day of travel and thought perhaps that was why I felt as I did; it would be different in the morning.

But the next morning a heavy, oppressive spirit still hung over the church. Worship never took off. No one was praising the Lord, and no spiritual gifts were being manifested.

Forty-five minutes of worship seem like an eternity when a sense of freedom and God's presence are not evident. At the end of the service I analyzed the situation. Maybe it's just that it's a morning service, and people are not fully awake yet, I thought. Tonight we'll have a real breakthrough.

The Wednesday evening service came, but no breakthrough came with it. By this time I was becoming very concerned. This is going to be a really long conference, I thought, if things do not change fast. I sought the Lord about how to break through this oppressive spirit.

As I led worship for the fourth time in the conference, the same pattern repeated itself. In the middle of worship, the Spirit of God spoke to me and said, "Have everyone shout, and tell them not to stop until you tell them to." So I told the congregation what the Lord had spoken to me. We shouted for twenty minutes. About ten minutes into the shouting something broke open in the spirit realm, and the oppressive spirit left.

In the midst of the shouting, the Lord gave me a vision of the heavenly host coming forth in pursuit of a demonic army in retreat. God was routing the enemy as we were shouting unto the Lord with the voice of triumph. God arose, and His enemies were scattered.

From that point on, there was freedom in the services. The worship was exciting as people entered into praise during each service. The gifts of the Spirit were manifested as people were healed, delivered and set free. But the release came as a result of the twenty minutes of shouting we did on Thursday morning.

I would like to close this chapter with the words of a song.

SHOUT, YE PEOPLE OF ZION

Shout, ye people of Zion,
Shout your praise to the King.
Shout, ye people of Zion,
As He leads us in victory;
For we are the army of God
With His praises upon our lips.
We are trampling down His enemies
As they become His footstool.[1]

EIGHT

JEHOSHAPHAT'S REVELATION

In 2 Chronicles 20 we read the account of what I call Jehoshaphat's dilemma. Three different armies had gathered together against Judah. Jehoshaphat, king of Judah, was faced with insurmountable odds. He was a "dead duck" unless God moved on his behalf.

"Alarmed, Jehoshaphat resolved to inquire of the Lord" (v. 3, NIV). He decided it was time to "seek the Lord while he may be found" (Is. 55:6, NIV).

As the people of Judah sought the Lord, the Spirit of the Lord came upon a temple musician named Jahaziel who prophesied the word of the Lord.

> And he said, Hearken ye, all Judah, and ye inhabitants of Jerusalem, and thou king Jehoshaphat. Thus saith the Lord unto you, Be not afraid nor dismayed by reason of this great multitude; for the battle is not yours, but God's. Tomorrow go ye down against them: behold, they come up by the cliff of Ziz; and ye shall find them at the end of the brook, before the wilderness of Jeruel. Ye shall not need to fight in this battle: set yourselves, stand ye still, and see the salvation of the Lord with you, O Judah and Jerusalem: fear not, nor be dismayed; tomorrow go out against them: for the Lord will be with you.
>
> And Jehoshaphat bowed his head with his face to the ground: and all Judah and the inhabitants of Jerusalem fell before the Lord, worshipping the Lord (2 Chron. 20:15-18).

Jahaziel prophesies battle instructions to the nation of Judah. He prophesies that they will not need to fight because God has a different plan of warfare for them. He also prophesies that they are to march out against the enemy on the next day.

As Jehoshaphat receives the prophetic strategy from the Lord on the following day, he gives the people a little pep talk.

Early in the morning they left for the Desert of Tekoa. As they set out, Jehoshaphat stood and said, "Listen to me, Judah and people of Jerusalem! Have faith in the Lord your God and you will be upheld; have faith in his prophets and you will be successful" (v. 20, NIV).

Then Jehoshaphat does one of the most unorthodox things ever done by a commander-in-chief of an army.

After consulting the people, Jehoshaphat appointed men to sing to the Lord and to praise him for the splendor of his holiness as they went out at the head of the army, saying: "Give thanks to the Lord, for his love endures forever" (v. 20:21, NIV).

Can you imagine this? He puts the band and the singers at the front of the army. Either God was going to do something great, or there would be no more music in the nation of Judah!

People volunteer to be on our church worship team. I wonder how many volunteers Jehoshaphat had that day. Their lives, in fact, depended on their worship. If it didn't prove to be successful there would be no second chance. What faith in the prophecy from Jahaziel these men had.

Then they proceeded to march out against their enemy with the praises of God in their mouths.

As they began to sing and praise, the Lord set ambushes against the men of Ammon and Moab and Mount Seir who were invading Judah, and they were defeated. The men of Ammon and Moab rose up against the men from Mount Seir to destroy and annihilate them. After they finished slaughtering the men from Seir, they helped to destroy one another. When the men of Judah came to the place that overlooks the desert and looked toward the vast army, they saw only dead bodies lying on the ground; no one had escaped. So Jehoshaphat and his men went to carry off their plunder, and they found among them a great amount of equipment and clothing and also articles of value — more than they could take away. There was so much plunder that it took three days to collect it (vv. 22-25, NIV).

A mighty victory was wrought as God's people sang praises unto the Lord. Singing praises unto the Lord causes confusion to come into the camp of the enemy. According to Bill Hamon, founder and president of Christian International Network of Prophetic Ministries, prophetic praise is God's jamming device to confuse the demonic spirit communication channels, thereby causing their destruction.[1] Jehoshaphat had a revelation of the power of praise.

It is interesting that they praised the Lord for His mercy and love. To be truthful, I could never understand why they would sing about the mercy of God. I asked the Lord about this, and He showed me Jehoshaphat's revelation.

Jehoshaphat's revelation of mercy was different from ours in the church today. We see mercy in the light of the cross and our redemption. Jesus had not come to the earth yet when Jehoshaphat lived. Therefore, his revelation of mercy was different from ours. The song the nation of Judah sang as they went out against their enemy gives us some insight into his revelation.

O give thanks unto the Lord; for he is good: for his mercy endureth forever. O give thanks unto the God of gods: for his mercy endureth forever. O give thanks to the Lord of lords: for his mercy endureth forever.

To him who alone doeth great wonders: for his mercy endureth forever. To him that by wisdom made the heavens: for his mercy endureth forever. To him that stretched out the earth above the waters: for his mercy endureth forever. To him that made great lights: for his mercy endureth forever: the sun to rule by day: for his mercy endureth forever: the moon and stars to rule by night: for his mercy endureth forever.

To him that smote Egypt in their firstborn: for his mercy endureth forever; and brought Israel from among them: for his mercy endureth forever: with a strong hand, and with a stretched out arm: for his mercy endureth forever.

To him which divided the Red sea into parts: for his mercy endureth forever: and made Israel to pass through the midst of it: for his mercy endureth forever: but overthrew Pharaoh and his host in the

Red sea: for his mercy endureth forever. To him which led his people through the wilderness: for his mercy endureth forever.

To him which smote great kings: for his mercy endureth forever: and slew famous kings: for his mercy endureth for ever: Sihon king of the Amorites: for his mercy endureth forever: and Og the king of Bashan: for his mercy endureth forever: and gave their land for an heritage: for his mercy endureth forever: even an heritage unto Israel his servant: for his mercy endureth forever.

Who remembered us in our low estate: for his mercy endureth forever: and hath redeemed us from our enemies: for his mercy endureth forever. Who giveth food to all flesh: for his mercy endureth forever. O give thanks unto the God of heaven: for his mercy endureth forever (Ps. 136).

Sung in responsive, alternating parts, this antiphonal song praises God for His love and mercy. Interestingly enough, over one-fourth of the song praises God for destroying the enemies of the people. Verses 10, 15 and 17-20 praise God directly for destroying their past enemies. Verses 11-14 and 24 praise God for His deliverance which resulted or culminated in the destruction of their enemies. Their revelation of God's mercy was that He would destroy their enemies. Their understanding of mercy was that their enemies did not have a chance.

The psalmist David had this same revelation and understanding of mercy when he wrote:

> And of thy mercy cut off mine enemies, and destroy all them that afflict my soul: for I am thy servant (Ps. 143:12).

David knew that God's mercy in action would be the destruction of all his enemies. Jehoshaphat realized God's mercy was militant.

Let me give you a natural example of mercy and love. We have a swing set in our backyard on which my children play. If a mean dog were to come into the yard while my children were playing and attack them, I would not try to discuss anything with the dog. Like any other father I would run outside and yell at that dog! I might even have something in my hand to "execute my judgment" upon that animal. And if I had to, I would kill the dog.

My actions against that animal are the result of showing mercy to my children. Because of my love for them I get angry when I see someone or something hurting them. I would be an unmerciful and unloving father if I did not act in this manner.

Jesus said, "If ye then, being evil, know how to give good gifts to your children, how much more shall your Father which is in heaven..." (Matt. 7:11). If we would destroy an animal that attacks our children, how much more will our heavenly Father war against the enemies of our souls?

Much of our understanding of mercy is not wrong; it is simply incomplete. I thank God for the cross and the blood of Jesus. But the revelation that Jehoshaphat and the children of Judah had was different from ours. We need to add Jehoshaphat's understanding of mercy and love to our own. Then, when we sing about the mercy of God, we will see the same results they experienced.

It is the understanding and revelation we possess that allow God's power to be released as we sing. There is no power in singing without biblical understanding and Holy Ghost illumination of what is being sung.

The Bible records another account of a mighty victory that was won as a result of singing praises to the Lord.

> And when they had laid many stripes upon them, they cast them into prison, charging the jailer to keep them safely: who, having received such a charge, thrust them into the inner prison, and made their feet fast in the stocks. And at midnight Paul and Silas prayed, and sang praises to God: and the prisoners heard them. And suddenly there was a great earthquake, so that the foundations of the prison were shaken: and immediately all the doors were opened, and everyone's bands were loosed (Acts 16:23-26).

As Paul and Silas praised the Lord, two noteworthy events occurred. First, the foundations of the prison were shaken. This has great spiritual significance. The devil desires to put people in the prison of darkness, despair, oppression, sickness and sin. After Paul and Silas sang praises, an earthquake shook the foundations of the prison. When we sing, the very foundations of the kingdom of darkness are shaken.

Second, after the foundations were shaken, the prison doors flew open, and everyone's bands were loosed. In the midst of Paul and Silas's singing of praises, people were set free. God's power is also manifested when we come together and sing to Him.

In May 1991 I was leading worship at a Christian International Conference in Pensacola, Florida. During one of the services a man's deaf ear popped open as we sang the second song. No one had laid hands on him or prayed for him. Thank God that in the midst of singing and rejoicing his "bands were loosed."

In January 1992 I was conducting a Prophetic Warfare Praise seminar in Columbia, South Carolina. We had dedicated the last night of the conference to waging war in the heavenlies with our praise. We had a tremendous breakthrough that night as we sang warfare songs. Many people gave their lives to Jesus as their "prison doors flew open" and their "bands were loosed."

> And he hath put a new song in my mouth,
> even praise unto our God: many shall see
> it, and fear, and shall trust in the Lord
> (Ps. 40:3).

As the people heard the praises to God, they put their trust in Him. The spirits that had blinded them to the gospel were pushed back as praise allowed their hearts to be wooed by the Holy Spirit.

Looking once again in 2 Chronicles 20 at the story of Jehoshaphat we see two statements by Jahaziel that we still hear in churches today. One is found in verse 15: "The battle is not yours, but God's." Some say it this way, "The battle belongs to the Lord." The other is found in verse 17: "Stand ye still, and see the salvation of the Lord." Many think these verses mean to do nothing. That is not correct. Immediately after Jahaziel prophesied that the battle was the Lord's, he said in verse 16, "Tomorrow go ye down against them."

Also, after he told them to stand still, he said in verse 17, "Tomorrow go out against them." The Spirit of God was saying to the nation of Judah that they were not going to have to fight with natural weapons of war. This battle was not going to be won by the sword, but by a different kind of warfare.

Likewise, we must realize there is a fight to be fought, but not with natural weapons. God has given us weapons of praise that have power against principalities and the devil. As we go forth singing the praises of God, our enemy is turned back in confusion.

If Jehoshaphat and the nation of Judah had not marched against their enemies singing praises unto the Lord, there would have been no victory.

As one minister says, "God is a fair checkers player. You move, and then He moves."

Unless we take up our weapons of praise, God cannot arise on our behalf and destroy our enemies. Let us go forth and sing the praises of our Lord as He brings confusion to the camp of the enemy, resulting in great victory.

NINE

CRUSHING THE HEAD OF THE SERPENT

We have received a lot of teaching and read numerous books on our position with Christ Jesus and our spiritual authority over the enemy. The Word of God declares that all things are under our feet (1 Cor. 15:25). It also declares that evil principalities and powers are spoiled (Is. 33:1). If all of this is true, why do we have to fight? Why do we have to war against a defeated foe?

First of all, we must understand the difference between legal position and living reality. Legally and positionally the devil has no authority over any child of God, yet he has caused oppression, sickness and sin. But that does not change the truth of God's Word.

We must learn to acquire that which is legally and positionally ours, bringing it into a living reality that we can experience. The same apostle Paul who wrote that "all things are under your feet" also wrote that we are to fight, war, wrestle and take up weapons of war. Although he wrote that principalities and powers are spoiled, he also wrote that we are still wrestling against them (Eph. 6:12). None of this will make sense to us until we realize the difference between legal position and living reality.

Our spiritual position in Christ Jesus enables us to bring forth the living reality of His victory. Praise, worship, prayer and the Word of God are the tools and weapons we use to bring positional truth into living reality.

In Romans 16:20 Paul writes, "The God of peace will soon crush Satan under your feet" (NIV). As I meditated upon this verse, I began to understand there is a difference between the devil's just being under my feet and his being crushed under my feet. I don't want the devil just under my feet; I want him crushed under my feet! How do we crush the devil under our feet?

> "But for you who revere my name, the sun of righteousness will rise with healing in its wings. And you will go out and *leap* like calves released from the stall. Then you will *trample* down the wicked; they will be

77

ashes under the soles of your feet on the day when I do these things," says the Lord Almighty (Mal. 4:2-3, NIV, emphasis added).

This Scripture verse refers to leaping like calves released from the stall. This is an analogy used to describe the way we are to rejoice before the Lord. If you have seen a rodeo, you can understand this. When the gate of the stall is opened, the bull jumps and leaps.

Malachi is prophesying that as we begin to leap and dance before the Lord in praise to His name, we will trample down the wicked. To trample something is to put it under our feet. We don't use our heads or hands to trample. We trample with our feet. So we trample the wicked (the devil) under our feet as we go out and leap like calves released. Webster's dictionary defines *trample* as "to crush as by treading heavily upon." The devil is crushed beneath our feet as we go forth with rejoicing and dancing.

Malachi goes on to say that the wicked "will be ashes under the soles of your feet" (v. 3). From this verse I believe we can see that we can do spiritual warfare with our feet as we leap and dance before the Lord. When we dance before the Lord, there is a purpose for doing so. We don't dance because it is the charismatic thing to do. We dance before the Lord because the Bible tells us to, and we crush the head of the serpent as we do so. We are dancing in celebration of the victory that we have won in Christ Jesus. Psalm 149:3 says, "Let them praise his name with dancing" (NIV).

This is not the only method we use to crush the

enemy. But dancing and rejoicing are scriptural means by which we can conduct spiritual warfare, thereby bruising the serpent's head.

In Ezekiel 28:11-19, we find a prophecy to Satan. God declares, "I will bring thee to ashes upon the earth" (v. 18). How is God going to bring the devil to ashes? I believe the church is the instrument God is using to accomplish this. According to Malachi 4:2-3, we will make the wicked — the devil — as ashes under our feet, as we go out and leap like calves released from the stall! As we go forth rejoicing and dancing we will see the devil brought to ashes.

Let us look at another Scripture passage concerning the relationship of praise and the treading down of our enemies.

> Mine anger was kindled against the shepherds, and I punished the goats: for the Lord of hosts hath visited his flock the *house of Judah*, and hath made them as his goodly horse in the battle...And they shall be as mighty men, which *tread down their enemies* in the mire of the streets in the battle: and they shall fight, because the Lord is with them, and the riders on horses shall be confounded (Zech. 10:3,5, emphasis added).

We know the name Judah means praise. Thus we see that God will make the people of praise, the house of Judah, like His royal horse in the battle. We are the horse that the Lord of hosts rides into battle. This passage goes on to state that the Lord and His people of praise will be like mighty men who tread down their enemies. As we praise God with our feet, they become instruments of war to tread upon the enemy's head.

For some reason the area of dance and expressive worship receive a lot of criticism from people who do not understand it. Some have created controversy with terms like "dancing in the Spirit" versus "dancing in the flesh." Being from a Pentecostal background, I understand what is being said. Most Pentecostal churches teach that you are not to dance before the Lord unless the "Spirit moves you." To dance deliberately as an act of your will is considered by many to be "in the flesh." Choreographed dance is equally thought to be "in the flesh."

I have never understood exactly why the feet get picked on. Perhaps it's because the enemy wants to keep us blinded to the power that is released as God's people praise Him with dancing.

In the book of James, the Bible refers to the tongue as the most defiled member of the body. Yet I have never heard anyone accused of "singing in the flesh"! How do we sing? We look at the words of the song, open our mouths and begin to sing without any prompting by the Holy Spirit. If we can do this with the most defiled member of the body, how much more can we deliberately, as an act of our wills, begin to dance before the Lord?

A religious spirit can cause a critical, judgmental attitude that accuses others of being in the flesh with their worship and praise. These kinds of accusations do not edify the body of Christ; they only foster confusion. God has called us to liberty (2 Cor. 3:17). Michal, Saul's daughter and David's wife, looked out on David as he danced before the Lord and disdained him for it (2 Sam. 6:16). The end result for her was barrenness. Our own ministries can become barren and unfruitful if we look at the praise and worship of others with a critical eye.

Michal was on the wrong side of the window. Instead of looking out on her husband, David, she could have been out there with him.

We find something very interesting in the account of Gideon's victory over the Midianites. After Gideon and his army blew the trumpets, broke the pitchers and gave up a shout, the Midianite army ran in terror. Some of the Midianite soldiers rose up against each other and killed one another.

> When the three hundred trumpets sounded, the Lord caused the men throughout the camp to turn on each other with their swords. The army fled to Beth Shittah toward Zererah as far as the border of Abel Meholah near Tabbath (Judg. 7:22, NIV).

The part of the army that fled ran as far as the border of Abel Meholah. In other words, final victory was realized at Abel Meholah. The name *Abel Meholah* means "meadow of the dance." As we go forth dancing and rejoicing before the Lord, our enemy, the devil, is crushed beneath our feet. We, the church, are a great army that is on the offensive. The devil is on the run. Let us pursue him to Abel Meholah and there trample him beneath our feet with rejoicing, dancing and praise!

TEN

EVERY STROKE WILL BE TO THE MUSIC

The voice of the Lord will shatter Assyria;
with his scepter he will strike them down.
Every stroke the Lord lays on them
with his punishing rod
will be to the music
of tambourines and harps,
as he fights them in battle
with the blows of his arm.
Isaiah 30:31-32, NIV, emphasis added

What a powerful Scripture passage! In this chapter I would like to examine the role of prophetic music in spiritual warfare. We have been taught that prophecy edifies, exhorts and comforts. We've had similar teaching that anointed music can minister to both the spirit and soul of man. I believe God wants us to see that the prophetic voice of the Lord and anointed prophetic music are

weapons of war to be used against our enemy.
When God called Jeremiah, He said,

> Now, I have put my words in your mouth.
> See, today I appoint you over nations and
> kingdoms to uproot and tear down, to de-
> stroy and overthrow, to build and to plant
> (Jer. 1:9-10, NIV).

Notice that four of the six things the word of the
Lord will do are destructive. The prophetic word
comes not only to edify and exhort us, but also to
uproot, tear down, destroy and overthrow the kingdom of darkness. The same word that blesses us
destroys the enemy. The prophetic word has power
to destroy the works of the enemy. That's why Paul
told Timothy to war a good warfare with the
prophecies spoken over him (1 Tim. 1:18). Obviously, Paul had a revelation of using the prophetic
word in spiritual warfare.
    With this in mind, let's look at the prophetic
song.

> Do not get drunk on wine, which leads to
> debauchery. Instead, be filled with the
> Spirit. Speak to one another with psalms,
> hymns and spiritual songs. Sing and make
> music in your heart to the Lord, always
> giving thanks to God the Father for every-
> thing, in the name of our Lord Jesus
> Christ (Eph. 5:18-20, NIV).

Paul lists three different categories of songs:
psalms, hymns and spiritual songs. I would like to
focus on the last one — *spiritual songs*. The literal

definition of a spiritual song is "ode of the Spirit" or "song of the Spirit." These are songs of praise, prophecy, warfare, healing and deliverance. They are prophetic in nature in the sense that they come forth spontaneously in an inspirational manner. They are also prophetic in the sense that God is singing through His church, expressing His mind, purpose and will. I can see six different types of prophetic or spiritual songs found in the Bible. I would like to discuss each one individually, paying particular attention to the last two.

Song of the Lord

The first is called the song of the Lord (2 Chron. 29:27). The song of the Lord is, literally, prophecy in song. It is "thus saith the Lord" coming forth through a song. It has the same purpose as prophecy, which is to edify, exhort and comfort (1 Cor. 14:3).

> The Lord thy God in the midst of thee is mighty; he will save, he will rejoice over thee with joy; he will rest in his love, he will joy over thee with singing (Zeph. 3:17).

This reveals that the Lord will rejoice over us with singing. Many do not realize that our God sings. He desires to sing to His church. In Psalm 91 we have an example of the song of the Lord. In the beginning of this psalm, the psalmist praises the Lord and declares that God is our fortress. But as he reaches the end of the psalm, the person singing changes.

"Because he loves me," says the Lord, "I will rescue him; I will protect him, for he acknowledges my name. He will call upon me, and I will answer him; I will be with him in trouble, I will deliver him and honor him. With long life will I satisfy him and show him my salvation" (Ps. 91:14-16, NIV).

Notice that it says, " 'Because he loves me,' says the Lord." The psalmist begins by singing to the Lord, but the Lord ends the psalm by singing to the psalmist. God declares prophetically to the psalmist through song what He will do. It is the Lord singing to His people.

SONG OF THE LORD (DIRECTED TO THE FATHER)

The second type of prophetic song is also the song of the Lord, but it is directed to the Father rather than to the church. This is an inspired prophetic song of praise, worship and adoration. Some call this the singing of a new song.

He says, "I will declare your name to my brothers; in the presence of the congregation I will sing your praises" (Heb. 2:12, NIV).

The verse refers to Jesus as He sings praise to the Father in the midst of the congregation. How will He do this? Through His body, the church.

Song of the Bridegroom

The third type of prophetic song is called the song of the bridegroom. In Revelation 19:7 the Bible refers to the church as the bride. The bridegroom is Jesus. We have a beautiful picture of the song of the bridegroom painted in the Song of Solomon. Most Bible scholars will agree that the Song of Solomon typifies the relationship between Christ and His church.

We see a picture of the bridegroom serenading His bride. The song of the bridegroom is much like the song of the Lord but is usually a love song to the bride and is then followed by the song of the bride.

> In the towns of Judah and the streets of Jerusalem that are deserted, inhabited by neither men nor animals, there will be heard once more the sounds of joy and gladness, *the voices of bride and bridegroom*, and the voices of those who bring thank offerings to the house of the Lord saying, "Give thanks to the Lord Almighty, for the Lord is good; his love endures forever" (Jer. 33:10-11, NIV, emphasis added).

Song of the Bride

This brings us to the fourth type of prophetic song called the song of the bride. This is a spontaneous prophetic song of love and adoration in response to the song of the bridegroom. This type of prophetic song is usually responsive in nature as the bride expresses to the bridegroom her love for

Him. It is also usually intimate in nature and enables the church to express by the Spirit of God the depth of love it has for the bridegroom, Jesus.

SONG OF DELIVERANCE

The fifth type of prophetic song is called the song of deliverance. This is a prophetic song of healing, deliverance and restoration. It is much like a word of knowledge in song.

> Thou art my hiding place; thou shalt preserve me from trouble; thou shalt compass me about with songs of deliverance (Ps. 32:7).

This type of song releases instantaneous manifestations of healing, miracles and deliverance. It is where the voice of the Lord, through song, begins to destroy the work of the enemy.

In June 1988 I was ministering in a Sunday evening service in Griffin, Georgia. After teaching on praise and worship I began to play the keyboard and lead the church in worship. As we worshipped, I sensed the Spirit of God prompting me to sing a song of deliverance. I mustered up enough faith and stepped out and sang, "There is someone here who was in an accident and misaligned the vertabrae in your neck. You have continual pain in that area. But now the hand of the Lord is upon you, and you are being set free and healed by the power of God."

I wasn't sure if I was right or not. I was acting on a slight impression of what I sensed in my spirit. At the end of the service, a woman in the back of the auditorium came to the front and shared with the pastor's wife what happened to her. She later told me the same story.

"I was in an automobile accident," she said, "and misaligned some vertebrae in my neck. I had continual pain to the point of having to take heavy medication to be able to cope. As you began to sing that song, it felt like warm hands were placed on the back of my neck. Something popped in my neck, and every bit of pain left me instantaneously."

The pastor was in one of our conferences later that year in October. We were riding in a van together when he asked me if I recalled that service with the lady who was healed. I told him yes. He said that the lady had experienced no pain since that night. Hallelujah! The voice of the Lord shattered the work of the enemy. The song of deliverance had accomplished its purpose. It brought healing and deliverance from the oppression of the enemy.

Prophetic Song of War

The sixth and last type of prophetic song is called the prophetic song of war. This song declares our victory in Christ Jesus. Its purpose is to wage spiritual warfare against principalities, powers, rulers of the darkness of this world and spiritual wickedness in the heavenly realms. It is directed toward our enemy and at times will even call out the name of a particular demonic power. It is a prophecy that is sung to demonic forces.

And you will *sing* as on the night you celebrate a holy festival; *your hearts will re-joice* as when people go up with flutes to the mountain of the Lord, to the Rock of Israel. The Lord will cause men to hear his majestic voice and will make them see his arm coming down with raging anger and consuming fire, with cloudburst, thunderstorm and hail. The *voice of the Lord will shatter Assyria*; with his scepter he will strike them down. Every stroke the Lord lays on them with his punishing rod *will be to the music of tambourines and harps, as he fights them in battle with the blows of his arm* (Is. 30:29-32, NIV, emphasis added).

This passage records that the Lord causes His voice to be heard in the midst of singing and rejoicing: "You will sing," and "your hearts will rejoice." In the midst of praise God will "cause men to hear His majestic voice."

Then Isaiah tells us what the voice of the Lord will do. "The voice of the Lord will shatter Assyria [the enemy]." As you read these verses together, you see a picture of God's voice being released through the prophetic song.

Let's explore this a little more. The King James Version reads like this: "For through the voice of the Lord shall the Assyrian be beaten down." Then Isaiah says by the Spirit of God that "every stroke...will be to the music" (v. 32, NIV). In other words, the prophetic voice of the Lord strikes and beats down the enemy as it is administered through music (or song).

He is talking about the prophetic song. The word

beaten is the Hebrew word *chathath*. It means "to prostrate" or "to break down by violence or by confusion and fear." This is what Isaiah declares the voice of the Lord will do. As we sing prophetically, strokes are laid upon our enemy. We bring confusion to the camp of the enemy through the prophetic song. Demonic forces are terrorized as we declare in song what the Spirit of God is saying.

I recall a particular service in which I was leading worship. It seemed as if no one was entering into the praise. Something seemed to be binding the people from praise. There was no liberty or freedom. I asked the Lord what to do. I sensed Him telling me to "sing prophetically."

"But, Lord, I don't have anything to sing prophetically," I replied.

"Open your mouth, and I will fill it," God said.

So I opened my mouth and sang, "For the Spirit of the Lord would say," and I proceeded to sing a prophetic song. Words flowed forth from my spirit as I acted in faith on what God had spoken to me. As the prophetic song came forth, the binding spirit was "beaten down." Freedom came into the service. The worship service ended with everyone praising the Lord with wild abandonment. It was glorious.

When God took Ezekiel to the valley of dry bones (Ezek. 37), Ezekiel saw the power of the prophetic word. God spoke to Ezekiel to prophesy to the bones. As he prophesied to them, the bones came together, muscle came on the bones, flesh came on them, and they stood up. He then prophesied for the wind to blow upon them, and they came forth as a great army. The prophetic word of the Lord has *resurrection power!* You may think your congregation is dead, but I guarantee that it's not as dead as Ezekiel's congregation was that day. The word of the Lord can breathe life into your worship service.

In another service Dr. Bill Hamon had called a special warfare praise and intercession service at Christian International. The ministry had come under the attack of a major principality. Jane Hamon, copastor of the Christian International Family Church, had prophetically received the name of the principality that was bringing the attack against us. The name was Rahabar.

At one point in the praise and worship we said corporately, "Rahabar, you are bound, and now you're coming down." We repeated this statement over and over with vehemence as the music played. We ended with a victory shout. The attack of the enemy ceased. We had stopped the enemy in his tracks, as we recited prophetically and sang to this principality with a revelation of what we were accomplishing.

Paul spoke of this in the third chapter of Ephesians.

> His intent was that now, *through the church,* the manifold wisdom of God should be made known to the rulers and authorities in the heavenly realms (Eph. 3:10, NIV, emphasis added).

Notice that it is through the church that the wisdom of God, or His word, is to be made known to the rulers in the heavenly realms. God has given us, the church, the responsibility of declaring His word prophetically to demonic powers and princi-

palities for the purpose of destroying their kingdom.

Let's look at the familar story of David and Goliath. As David went out to meet the Philistine
giant, he said to him:

> You come against me with sword and
> spear and javelin, but I come against you
> in the name of the Lord Almighty, the God
> of the armies of Israel, whom you have de-
> fied. *This day* the Lord will hand you over
> to me, and I'll strike you down and cut off
> your head. *Today* I will give the carcasses
> of the Philistine army to the birds of the
> air and the beasts of the earth, and the
> whole world will know that there is a God
> in Israel. All those gathered here will
> know that it is not by sword or spear that
> the Lord saves; for the battle is the Lord's,
> and he will give all of you into our hands
> (1 Sam. 17:45-47, NIV, emphasis added).

I do not believe this was a faith confession. I
believe something rose up inside David, and he began to prophesy to the giant. Notice he said, "This
day...." David got specific. There is no margin for
error when you get that specific. But I thank God
that David had the word of the Lord for the giant.

The Philistine giant is a type of the enemy we
face. God wants us to arise and prophesy to the
demonic "bully" that is trying to push us around.
Even though the battle was the Lord's, David still
had to go out and face the giant, sling the stone
and cut off his head. God causes us to triumph, but,
like David, *we must go out and fight!*

We can derive another mighty truth from this story. As David declared, "The whole world will know that there is a God in Israel." When would the world know? After he slayed Goliath! Do you know when the world is going to know there is a God in the church? When we arise in the power of the Spirit, as the great and mighty army that Ezekiel prophesied about, and slay the spiritual giants that are trying to rule the earth.

We must remind ourselves that people do not believe in Jesus because they have been blinded by demonic spirits (2 Cor. 4:4). Spiritual warfare should precede the preaching of the Word; people will be saved when they are no longer blinded by evil spirits.

A New Testament example of this is found in the book of Acts. Paul and Barnabas had traveled to the island of Cyprus. Upon reaching the island they traveled from one end to the other. Arriving in the city of Paphos, they met a Jewish sorcerer and false prophet named Bar-jesus. This man was an attendant of the proconsul Sergius Paulus. The proconsul wanted to hear the gospel, so he sent for Paul and Barnabas. Bar-jesus was obviously not thrilled about this and opposed Paul and Barnabas.

> Then Saul, (who also is called Paul,) filled with the Holy Ghost, set his eyes on him, and said, O full of all subtlety and all mischief, thou child of the devil, thou enemy of all righteousness, wilt thou not cease to pervert the right ways of the Lord? And now, behold, the hand of the Lord is upon thee, and thou shalt be blind, not seeing

> the sun for a season. And immediately there fell on him a mist and a darkness; and he went about seeking some to lead him by the hand. Then the deputy, when he saw what was done, believed, being astonished at the doctrine of the Lord (Acts 13:9-12).

Bar-jesus represents the spirits of false religion and the antichrist. Paul looks at him and prophesies the word of the Lord to him. The Spirit of God arose within Paul, and he pronounced a prophetic judgment upon Bar-jesus.

Again, we see the principle of prophesying to demonic principalities and powers. This man Bar-jesus was practicing the same thing that the "New" Age false prophets are propagating today. We can expect to see some of the same things happen to them that happened to Bar-jesus.

I would like you to see the results of this prophetic word: "Then the deputy when he saw what was done, believed" (v. 12). Paul's prophetic declaration resulted in a demonstration of the power of God which made a believer out of the deputy. He knew that almighty God was with Paul. Recall what David said to Goliath: "I am going to kill you today and 'the whole world will know that there is a God in Israel.'"

Another example of prophesying to wicked principalities and powers is found in Exodus 5. Pharaoh is a type of the enemy that holds people in bondage.

> And afterward Moses and Aaron went in, and told Pharaoh, Thus saith the Lord

God of Israel, Let my people go, that they
may hold a feast unto me in the wilderness (5:1).

Here we see Moses and Aaron going before Pharaoh and giving him the word of the Lord. I am
giving all these scriptural examples to establish
the validity of the principle of prophesying to demonic powers. Many times in our worship services
we have sung prophetically to demonic principalities. In these songs we executed the judgment that
was written upon them (Ps. 149:9).

We have seen great things happen as a result of
the prophetic songs of war. At times, these songs
come forth in an antiphonal, or responsive, manner. Military squads march to antiphonal singing.
The word *antiphonal* is derived from two words:
anti and *phonal*. Anti means "against," and phonal
means "sound." In prophetic antiphonal singing we
literally sound against the principalities and powers of the air.

God desires to speak, and He wants His voice to
be heard. The apostle Paul said, "Covet to prophesy" (1 Cor. 14:39). The Spirit of God would not
have conveyed this through Paul if it were something we could not do. Let us release the voice of
the Lord through the prophetic song. The church
will be edified and blessed, and the kingdom of
darkness will be terrorized and depressed. Let us
move into the prophetic song with confidence and
faith, realizing that God's Spirit will be released
with power as we do so.

ELEVEN

THE PURPOSE OF WARFARE SONGS

Every move of God has produced new songs and choruses that declare what is being preached and taught. We are in the midst of a prophetic move of God. He is bringing forth in this hour a great company of prophets and prophetic songwriters. The trumpet is sounding, and the troops are assembling as they hear the word of the Lord. Spiritual warfare is one of those messages.

I believe in having a purpose for everything I do. Without it I accomplish nothing. When I first began writing songs, I wrote aimlessly. I would write whatever came to me in moments of inspiration. As I continued, the Lord was faithful in teaching me how to write. He also spoke to me about stirring up the prophetic songwriting gift within me. Since then I've written several hundred songs.

Now not only has God shown me His purpose for me at this time — to write warfare songs — but He also shows me the purpose, or purposes, of each song.

Why do we need to sing aggressive, confrontational, militant songs? Why can't we just sing sweet songs about the love of Jesus? These are valid questions which I will try to answer from the Bible and give some personal experiences and observations.

Colossians 3 contains the first two purposes for warfare songs:

> Let the word of Christ dwell in you richly in all wisdom; teaching and admonishing one another in psalms and hymns and spiritual songs, singing with grace in your hearts to the Lord (Col. 3:16).

The first purpose is to teach us biblical truth about spiritual warfare. Warfare music usually contains verses that speak of spiritual warfare, including some that may be unfamiliar. They declare our victory in Jesus Christ, while at the same time making us aware that we are still wrestling and fighting against demonic forces. Warfare songs speak of the army of the Lord going out to battle

97

against our enemy. An army's purpose is to fight.

Warfare songs may challenge a person's religious indoctrination. Every warfare song I have written can be validated with numerous Scripture verses. We should first investigate the whole Word of God, not just selected verses.

A second purpose for warfare music is to admonish one another. The word *admonish* means "to put in mind." In other words, once we are established in the truth of spiritual warfare, we then stir up our remembrance as we sing our songs. We put these truths in our minds through the singing of warfare songs. Notice what Peter said:

> Wherefore I will not be negligent to put you always in remembrance of these things, though you know them, and be established in the present truth (2 Peter 1:12).

Once you are established in the present truth of spiritual warfare and warfare praise, you must still have your memory stirred up. Singing of warfare songs accomplishes this.

A third purpose for warfare songs is to exhort. To exhort in the Greek means "to call near" or "to call for." It also means "to give a charge." As we sing these songs, we call for the army of the Lord to come forth. We call near all the warriors.

> Proclaim this among the nations: Prepare for war! Rouse the warriors! Let all the fighting men draw near and attack (Joel 3:9, NIV).

We, the church, are not a bless-me club. We are an army that is in a war against the devil and his demonic forces. An army assembles its troops.

I know of many intercession groups that play prophetic warfare praise tapes before they pray. The music stirs them up to war in the spirit. Thus we see how warfare music exhorts.

The fourth purpose for warfare songs is to release people in praise to the Lord. One of the main Hebrew words translated *praise* is *halal*. This word means "to declare, to make a show, boast, to be clamorously foolish." When we sing a song such as "Mighty Man of War," we declare that our God is a warrior. That is praising the Lord. Songs that speak of our victory in Christ or of overcoming the devil are praise to the Lord.

When we say the word *praise*, most people think of the book of Psalms. It is very interesting to read some of the psalms that the warrior David wrote by the Spirit of God. Some of those psalms praise God for killing wicked kings — even calling them by name! Many of the psalms contain statements that beseech the Lord to destroy people, break their teeth, cut off their seed, strike people with terror, clothe them with shame or bring coals upon their heads. The warfare songs we have written today are actually mild compared to some that David wrote. Yet no one would dispute that those psalms can be used to praise the Lord.

Warfare songs praise the Lord. God is glorified as we sing what is contained in His Word. A song does not have to be a vertical song — one directed to God — to be praise to Him. Songs that speak of who we are as the army of the Lord and what that army is doing are praise.

A fifth purpose for warfare songs is that they unite us against a common enemy. During the Gulf War and Operation Desert Storm unity in the United States seemed to be high. A common enemy and a common goal will always rally and unite people. We are exposing the enemy as we sing warfare songs. Instead of using the sword on our brothers or sisters, we realize that our swords have the devil's name on the blade.

Although the United States and the former USSR were diametrically opposed to each other, they became allies against Nazi Germany during World War II. When a common enemy exists, differences no longer matter. During the Gulf War we saw a nation considered to be predominantly Christian — the USA — join forces with several Islamic nations to fight against another Islamic nation — Iraq. The only thing that made this possible was the common-enemy principle. As we, the church, come into this revelation of a common enemy, we will see greater unity and victory. Warfare songs play a key role in developing this unity.

A sixth purpose for warfare songs is the release of corporate warfare.

> That the communication of thy faith may become effectual by the acknowledging of every good thing which is in you in Christ Jesus (Philem. 6).

I believe the key phrase in this verse is "may become effectual by the acknowledging." The acknowledging of biblical truths causes them to become effective. That is a spiritual principle that applies even to salvation. It is the acknowledging of Jesus as Lord that causes salvation to become effective in the heart of the believer (Rom. 10:9-10). It is the acknowledging of your sin and Jesus' blood that cause forgiveness of sins to become effective (1 John 1:9).

As we corporately acknowledge the Lord as a warrior, that character attribute of God becomes effective in our lives. He rises in us as the mighty warrior. Along with that, in the spirit realm angelic beings go forth and fight as they hearken to the "voice of his word" (Ps. 103:20).

As we acknowledge the warfare taking place in the spirit realm, our spiritual warfare through praise becomes more effective. A corporate force is released into the heavenlies, pulling down strongholds and scattering demonic principalities.

The last purpose for warfare songs is to declare in song what the Holy Spirit is saying to the church. In the prophetic movement, the church has figuratively crossed over the Jordan and entered the promised land. Now is the time to kill the giants in the land. Jordan has rolled back behind us, and there is nowhere to go but forward! The manna has ceased, and now we must go milk the cows and rob the beehives in order to have milk and honey.

The prophets are calling for the army of the Lord to come forth. The prophetic words are declaring that we, the church, must take up our weapons of war and fight.

I have purposed in my heart to write what the Spirit of God is declaring today. He wants us to sing forth His words. As we do, we will see the release of God's power and anointing through the church and the destruction of the kingdom of darkness.

TWELVE

ADVANCE AND OCCUPY

We have seen repeatedly how praise was used as a weapon of warfare. Throughout God's Word the Spirit of God demonstrated to us that praise and worship are more than words and music. Our praise has power to destroy and demolish the kingdom of darkness.

What is written and declared in the Bible is there for our admonition and instruction. The accounts that we read are there for us to follow. God has given the church a powerful weapon of war. That weapon is the high praises of God in our mouths.

It is time for the church to arise out of passivity and move into a dimension of militancy against the powers of hell. With the praises of God on our lips we take possession of what God has declared is already ours. We drive out the demonic principalities that have subjugated our rightful possessions and proceed to advance and occupy our land.

With our praise we silence the enemy. His plans fail as he lacks the power to carry them out. Uninhibited worship torments the enemy of our soul. The joyful sound of praise causes shock waves to be felt throughout the kingdom of darkness.

With our praise we execute the vengeance of our God upon the head of our enemy the devil. The principalities and powers that Jesus spoiled are bound with chains and with fetters of iron (Ps. 149:8). The judgments that almighty God has declared in His Word are enforced as His glorious praise goes forth.

Our plowshares are beaten into swords as we receive the revelation of the Spirit. Our praise then becomes a mighty sword we wield against our foe. No longer do we worship without purpose, but we worship with a revelation of the power of our praise. We sing with purpose and authority while understanding who we are as the body of Christ.

In the midst of our praise, the mighty man of war arises. He fights with us as we extol the greatness of His name. His zeal is stirred against our enemies as we shout joyfully to Him. He marches out to battle, like a warrior sounding the battle cry, as the sound of exaltation comes forth from His people.

God has declared that He inhabits the praises of His people. His presence is manifested in the midst of a worshipping priesthood of believers. He has revealed Himself throughout His Word as the Lord of hosts. He is the Lord of warriors. This mighty warrior is enthroned in our praises. In that habitation of praise He fights with and for us.

Every expression of our praise has a purpose. Every act of praise affects the realm of the spirit. For every action there is an equal and corresponding reaction in the unseen realm. We are not just making a lot of noise.

As we shout to God with the voice of triumph, God arises and His enemies are scattered. Satan's strongholds are broken up. The kingdom he has built is marred by the high praises of God that are released with shouts of joy.

Confusion and destruction are released into the enemy's camp as we go forth singing the songs of Zion. As Jehoshaphat and the people went out singing about the mercy of God, God's mercy was manifested in the destruction of their enemy. Likewise, as we sing with revelation, God manifests that revelation in our lives.

God is the creator of music. He is the original designer of musical instruments. His most beautiful angel, Lucifer, was created with musical instruments built into his body. Because of pride, Lucifer fell, and his music became perverted. The responsibility of filling the heavenlies with anointed music is now in the hands of the church. David, the man after God's own heart, created a multitude of musical instruments. As we play upon musical instruments in praise and honor of our Lord, the force of God's anointing and power is released, causing the enemy to run in terror.

God's voice is released and heard through prophecy as people praise Him. For every acceptable sacrifice of praise there is always a divine response. God responds to our worship by speaking to us by way of the prophetic word. God's voice is often released through the prophetic song as He rejoices over us with singing. The enemies of God are shattered as His mighty voice is heard. Healing, deliverance and restoration take place as the prophetic song is brought forth.

It is time for us to sing the war songs of Zion. The church has not been called to sit idly among our blessings, but rather to raise up a standard against the forces of darkness. We have been called to show forth His praises. Our songs should reflect our militant stand against the devil. As we sing strong, militant, warfare songs, corporate warfare is released in the heavenly realms. We admonish one another to be strong in the Lord and fight the good fight of faith.

This is not the day to retreat. This is the day to advance. We are not just holding on, but we are possessing. We will not just survive, but we are taking over. We are subduing the kingdom of darkness by declaring the kingdom of God. Let us take up all the weaponry that God has laid at our disposal, including the weapon of praise. We have been called to the kingdom for such an hour as this to silence the enemy.

NOTES

FOREWORD

1. Bill Hamon, *Prophets and the Prophetic Movement* (Shippensburg, Pa.: Destiny Image Publishers, 1990).

CHAPTER 7

1. Robert Gay, "Shout, Ye People of Zion," copyright © 1988, Prophetic Praise Ministries.

CHAPTER 8

1. Bill Hamon, *Prophets and the Prophetic Movement* (Shippensburg, Pa.: Destiny Image Publishers, 1990).

For more information
on resource products, such as
teaching tapes, worship tapes,
sound tracks and music,
or for ministry scheduling,
write or call:

Robert L. Gay
Prophetic Praise Ministries Inc.
1610 Rhode Island Ave.
Lynn Haven, FL 32444
(904) 265-1889

If you enjoyed *Silencing the Enemy*,
we would like to recommend the following books:

Taking Our Cities for God
by John Dawson
This national best-seller gives you Bible-based strategies and
tactics for winning your city for God. Author John Dawson shows
you how to discover God's purpose for your city, discern and break
spiritual strongholds and take the five steps to victory.

Public Praise
by Graham Kendrick
Graham Kendrick's powerful book will cause you to
flood your life and your city with praise and prayer.
This book explains the spiritual dynamics of praise marching
and chronicles the beginnings of what could be one of the
most significant movements of our generation.

The House of the Lord
by Francis Frangipane
In this challenging book Francis Frangipane shows believers
how to lay aside individual difficulties and doctrines
and come together in worship and warfare — to rebuild
the house of the Lord and bring healing to their cities.

Prayerwalking
by Graham Kendrick and Steve Hawthorne
This insightful book expounds on the dynamics of
advancing the cause of Christ in our neighborhoods and cities.
Authors Steve Hawthorne and Graham Kendrick
encourage systematic "prayerwalking" and teach believers
how to pray on-site with insight for their communities.

Available at your local Christian bookstore or from:

Creation House
600 Rinehart Road
Lake Mary, FL 32746
1-800-283-8494